The 30-Day Decluttering Breakthrough

Master the Art of Decluttering and Experience the Joy of a Transformed Life: A Proven, Step-by-Step Decluttering Challenge to Break Free from Chaos and Create a Sanctuary of Peace and Clarity

Seraphine Silverwood

Contents

Introduction

Welcome to the transformative journey of decluttering! In this chapter, we will embark on an uplifting exploration of the power of decluttering and its impact on your life. We'll delve into the concept of decluttering and how it extends far beyond just tidying up physical spaces. Get ready to embrace a new mindset and experience a positive shift in your mental, emotional, and even spiritual well-being.

Decluttering is not just about cleaning up and organizing physical spaces; it is a holistic practice that encompasses freeing yourself from unnecessary physical and mental burdens. It involves making deliberate choices to let go of possessions, thoughts, and habits that no longer serve a purpose in your life.

The presence of clutter in our environment can have a profound impact on our emotional and psychological well-being. Studies have shown that living amidst disorganization and excess can lead to increased stress, anxiety, and even feelings of overwhelm. Additionally, clutter has been linked to a decrease in focus and productivity, hindering our ability to fully engage with the present moment. By clearing away the physical chaos, we can create space for positivity and tranquility to flourish. This act of simplifying can extend to our mental and emotional states, allowing us to cultivate a sense of calm and clarity within ourselves. Letting go of physical belongings can also symbolize releasing emotional attachments, enabling us to move forward with a lighter heart.

The rewards of decluttering extend far beyond a tidy living space. A clutter-free environment can lead to improved physical health, as it reduces the presence of allergens and promotes better airflow. Moreover, the act of decluttering can also unearth forgotten treasures, reigniting joy and gratitude in our lives. On a deeper level, the process of decluttering empowers us to focus on what truly matters. By eliminating distractions and excess, we can cultivate an environment that fosters creativity, inspiration, and inner peace. The result is an uplifting and nurturing space that supports our well-being and personal growth.

The 30-day timeframe for this decluttering challenge is not arbitrary. Research suggests that it takes approximately 21 to 30 days to form a new habit. By committing to a month-long journey, you are laying the foundation for lasting change, allowing new habits and perspectives to take root in your life. Additionally, the 30-day challenge provides a structured and manageable approach to decluttering. It breaks down the process into smaller, achievable tasks, preventing overwhelm and enabling you to make steady progress toward your goals.

Before embarking on this transformative adventure, it's essential to prepare yourself mentally and gather the necessary tools. Begin by cultivating a positive mindset and embracing the potential for growth and renewal that decluttering offers. Equipping yourself with practical resources, such as storage containers, labeling materials, and donation boxes, can streamline the decluttering process. Additionally, consider seeking support from friends or family members who can provide encouragement and accountability throughout your journey.

Establishing clear intentions for this decluttering challenge will guide your efforts and keep you focused on the desired outcomes. Take the time to reflect on what you hope to achieve through decluttering. You may aspire to create a more peaceful and harmonious home, increase your productivity and efficiency, or simply experience a sense of liberation from overwhelming clutter. By setting intentions, you anchor your commitment to the journey and infuse your actions with purpose and meaning. Your intentions will serve as guiding lights, leading you toward a life that is aligned with your true values and aspirations.

The 30-day decluttering plan is designed to guide you through a systematic and transformative process. Each phase of the challenge will focus on a specific aspect of decluttering, gradually leading you toward a harmonious and clutter-free environment. During the 30-day journey, you will explore various areas of your life, including physical spaces, digital clutter, and mental habits. By addressing clutter on multiple levels, you will experience comprehensive and lasting change, setting the stage for a more fulfilling and intentional way of living. As we embark on this uplifting journey of transformation, remember that a clutter-free life is within your reach. Embrace the power of decluttering, and let's embark on this incredible journey together!

Chapter 1

Understanding Your Clutter - Identifying the Root Causes

Discovering Your Emotional Connections - Sentimental Clutter Unveiled

We often find ourselves holding onto sentimental items out of an emotional attachment that transcends mere practicality. These objects, laden with memories and meaning, can become anchors that tie us to the past. While it's natural to cherish moments and possessions that are dear to our hearts, it's important to remember that we carry the essence of these sentiments within us, not in the physical objects themselves. The process of decluttering sentimental items is not about diminishing their significance, but rather about honoring and fully embracing the emotions they represent. By delicately exploring the reasons behind holding onto these items, we can gently guide ourselves towards releasing them with love and gratitude. Each item holds a story, a memory, or a feeling. As we reminisce and reflect, we can acknowledge the impact they've had on our lives. This mindful reflection paves the way for us to realize that we're capable of treasuring these emotions within us, independent of the physical objects. By doing so, we liberate ourselves from the weight of clutter, allowing space for new experiences, growth, and memories. Let's foster a spirit of gratitude as we honor the sentimental items that have woven into the tapestry of our lives. With each embrace, each photograph, each memento, we can bid adieu with love and appreciation, knowing that the essence of what they represent will forever remain within us. In this process, we open ourselves up to new adventures, unencumbered by the shadows of the past. Through this act of loving release, we invite more light, joy, and abundance into our lives. As we embark on this journey of decluttering sentimental items, let us affirm that the memories and emotions remain eternally cherished within our hearts. By decluttering with mindfulness, we create space for greater fulfillment, harmony, and serenity. Embracing the abundance of beautiful memories within us, we step forward with grace and gratitude, ready to welcome new chapters of our lives.

Breaking Free from Procrastination - Taking the First Step

Procrastination, the thief of time, has often held us back from achieving our full potential. It lures us into a false sense of security, offering fleeting relief while gradually leading us away from our goals and dreams. But fear not, dear reader, for breaking free from procrastination begins with acknowledging its presence in our lives. The first step is to recognize that procrastination is merely a hurdle - a hurdle that can be overcome with dedication and self-awareness. Each day presents an opportunity to make progress, no matter how small. By taking that initial step, you are already on the path to reclaiming control of your time and energy. Embrace the exhilarating feeling of taking charge and moving forward, and watch as the momentum propels you closer to your aspirations. Remember, the journey of a thousand miles begins with a single step. You have the power within you to conquer procrastination and seize the day. So, let us embark on this transformative expedition together, celebrating each step forward with unwavering optimism and courage. As you set your sights on a procrastination-free horizon, envision the accomplishments and triumphs that await you. Visualize the joy and fulfillment that come with harnessing your productivity and embracing proactive habits. Break free from the restraints of delay, and embrace the liberating freedom of decisive action. Every moment is an opportunity to align with your purpose and pursue your ambitions. With each task completed, feel the sense of accomplishment wash over you, fueling your determination to persist in the face of procrastination's allure. This is your journey towards empowerment and resilience, and it begins by daring to take that courageous first step. As you navigate this empowering transformation, revel in the newfound clarity and vitality that accompany your proactive choices, illuminating the path ahead. You are capable, you are unstoppable, and you are worthy of a life free from the constraints of procrastination. Embrace the present moment, seize every opportunity, and savor the boundless possibilities that unfold when you choose to overcome procrastination. Your journey towards embracing proactive momentum is a testament to your unwavering commitment to personal growth and perseverance. Together, let us celebrate the dawn of a new era, where productivity triumphs over procrastination, and your aspirations materialize through consistent, purposeful actions.

Overcoming Decision Fatigue - Simplify Your Choices

In the journey of decluttering and simplifying our lives, one significant hurdle we often face is decision fatigue. This state of mental exhaustion and overwhelm arises from the countless choices we encounter daily. From the moment we wake up to the time we retire to bed, we are bombarded with decisions, big and small. Amidst this deluge, it's easy to feel drained and disheartened, leading to procrastination and stagnation in our decluttering efforts.

To overcome decision fatigue and simplify your choices, it's essential to embrace intentional living. Begin by understanding your core values and priorities. When you are clear about what truly matters to you, decision-making becomes more straightforward. Consider creating a vision board or journaling about your aspirations to reinforce your focus and reduce the mental clutter that arises from conflicting desires.

Another effective strategy is to establish routines and rituals that minimize the need for constant decision-making. By automating certain aspects of your day, such as meal planning, outfit selection, or morning rituals, you free up mental space for more significant decisions pertaining to decluttering and lifestyle changes.

Moreover, developing a 'less is more' mindset can significantly alleviate decision fatigue. Embrace the concept of minimalism not only in material possessions but also in your daily commitments and activities. Learn to say no to non-essential obligations, and streamline your schedule to create breathing room for spontaneity and relaxation. This intentional curation of your life empowers you to make authentic choices aligned with your well-being.

As you progress in simplifying your choices, consider the elimination of decision points by reducing unnecessary options. For instance, declutter your wardrobe to feature only items that align with your style and comfort, thus streamlining the process of getting dressed each day. Apply this principle to various aspects of your life, recognizing that having fewer options can lead to increased satisfaction and decisiveness.

Ultimately, this journey towards overcoming decision fatigue is an uplifting one. It allows you to reclaim your mental energy and direct it towards sculpting a life filled with purpose and joy. Through intentional living, embracing simplicity, and minimizing unnecessary choices, you pave the way for a decluttered existence that is in harmony with your truest self.

Consumerism Consciousness - Transform Your Buying Habits

Buying things can often be an exhilarating experience, but it's essential to consider the long-term impact of our purchases. By nurturing a conscious consumerism mindset, we can not only declutter our physical space but also enrich our lives in countless ways. A mindful approach to consumption begins with understanding the difference between our needs and wants. This distinction lays the foundation for transforming our buying habits into deliberate and fulfilling choices. Instead of being swayed by impulse or societal pressure, we can embrace a more intentional and gratifying mode of acquiring belongings.

Part of this process involves evaluating how our possessions align with our values and contribute to our overall well-being. We have the power to select items that resonate with our authentic selves, reflecting our aspirations and passions. Recognizing the value of experiences over material accumulation becomes second nature as we shift our focus towards a life filled with joyful moments and meaningful connections. Embarking on this journey enables us to appreciate the significance of each purchase while minimizing unnecessary acquisitions.

Moreover, cultivating consumerism consciousness invites us to explore alternative means of fulfillment beyond material possessions. We begin to seek satisfaction in immaterial treasures such as knowledge, personal growth, and shared experiences. This shift elevates our perspective, allowing us to savor the richness of life without relying solely on external objects. As a result, we become adept at discerning which investments truly amplify our happiness and serve a purpose in our lives, fostering a sustainable and fulfilling existence.

By adopting a conscious consumerism approach, we can also contribute to building a more sustainable and equitable world. Choosing to support ethical and environmentally responsible brands complements our effort to minimize clutter and uphold our values. Through these conscious choices, we play an active role in advocating for a harmonious coexistence with the planet and uplifting communities around the globe. Our purchasing decisions hold significant potential to drive positive change, and it's immensely empowering to realize the impact we can make through thoughtful consumption.

In essence, embracing a consumerism consciousness encompasses a profound transformation that extends far beyond our immediate surroundings. It empowers us to align our actions with our values, fosters genuine fulfillment, and positions us as catalysts for a brighter future. With each mindful purchase, we shape a narrative of purpose, compassion, and mindfulness, fueling a life enriched by meaningful experiences and lightened by clutter-free spaces.

Embracing the Freedom of Letting Go

Letting go is a powerful act of self-liberation that paves the way for a life filled with lightness and joy. When we release ourselves from the burden of excess possessions, we open the door to an abundance of positivity and peace. Embracing the freedom of letting go allows us to create space for new opportunities, experiences, and meaningful connections. It's an opportunity to rid ourselves of the unnecessary and make room for what truly matters. This process fosters a profound sense of empowerment, as we regain control over our environment and, consequently, over our lives. Each item we let go of becomes a stepping stone toward a bolder, more authentic existence. Embracing this journey requires a shift in mindset – a conscious decision to prioritize emotional well-being, mental clarity, and spiritual nourishment over material accumulation. It's about understanding that true richness lies in the intangible - in cherished memories, personal growth, and human connection. As you embark on this liberating endeavor, remind yourself that letting go is not a loss, but a gain. Pave your path with gratitude for the lessons learned from each possession released, and embrace the newfound space as an opportunity for renewal and rejuvenation. Revel in the exhilaration that comes with shedding the weight of clutter, and celebrate the freedom found in simplicity. By embracing the freedom of letting go, you beckon a life filled with purpose, light, and endless possibilities.

Clutter as a Shield - Understanding Stress and Trauma Responses

When we delve into the world of clutter, we often uncover a hidden layer of emotional attachment and protection. Clutter can serve as a shield, providing a sense of security and familiarity in times of stress or trauma. It's important to recognize that clutter accumulation can be a response to past experiences, serving as a protective barrier against external pressures. Understanding this aspect allows us to approach decluttering with empathy and self-compassion.

As we navigate through life, we encounter various stressors and challenging situations. In these moments, clutter can manifest as a coping mechanism, shielding us from the discomfort and uncertainty that accompany adversity. Whether it stems from past traumas or current stressors, clutter often represents an attempt to create a bubble of safety within our surroundings.

However, while clutter may initially provide a sense of comfort, it can also perpetuate a cycle of stress and anxiety. Acknowledging clutter as a shield prompts us to explore healthier coping strategies that align with our growth and well-being. By recognizing the underlying reasons for clutter accumulation, we empower ourselves to address the root causes and cultivate a nurturing environment that supports our emotional and mental health.

By embracing this understanding, we embark on a journey of healing and transformation. Letting go of clutter signifies a profound shift towards prioritizing our inner peace and resilience. As we release the shield of clutter, we step into a space of liberation, opening ourselves to new possibilities and experiences. Each item we part with becomes a symbol of our commitment to self-nurturing and a testament to our strength in facing challenges head-on.

In embracing this shift, we foster a mindset of abundance, drawing upon the positive energy that flows through a decluttered environment. The act of releasing clutter not only clears physical space but also creates room for optimism and fulfillment. Letting go becomes an empowering and uplifting process, representing a conscious choice to cultivate joy, serenity, and harmony in our lives.

With a compassionate heart, we honor the role clutter has played as a shield, acknowledging its protective intent. As we extend gratitude for the lessons learned, we embrace this pivotal moment of self-discovery and renewal. Through this transformative perspective, each step toward decluttering becomes a celebration of our resilience, inviting abundance and tranquility into our lives.

Spotting the Clutter Hotspots - Assess and Address

One of the key steps in decluttering your life is to identify the areas where clutter tends to accumulate. These 'clutter hotspots' may vary from person to person, but often include spaces such as the entrance hallway, kitchen countertops, and closets. By recognizing these areas, you can strategically address the root causes of clutter and create a more harmonious living environment. Begin by taking a mindful walk through your home, observing the areas that seem to collect excess items or feel chaotic. It's important to approach this process with curiosity and compassion, without self-judgment. Once you've identified the hotspots, take a moment to assess why clutter accumulates in those specific areas. Is it due to lack of organization, emotional attachments to certain items, or simply a habit of leaving things there out of convenience? Understanding the reasons behind the clutter allows you to address them effectively. Next, set aside dedicated time to tackle each hotspot. Start with one area at a time, and begin sorting through the items. As you make decisions about what to keep, donate, or discard, embrace the opportunity to create intentional choices for your space. Consider the purpose and significance of each item, and whether it aligns with your vision of a joyful, clutter-free environment. Utilize organizing containers, shelves, and storage solutions to optimize the functionality of these spaces. Engage in a joyful decluttering process by playing uplifting music, lighting scented candles, or inviting a friend to join you. Transforming clutter hotspots into rejuvenating spaces can be a rewarding experience that enhances your overall well-being. Lastly, remember to celebrate your progress. Revel in the newfound clarity and freedom that comes with addressing these clutter hotspots, knowing that you are creating a home that supports and uplifts you.

Mindful Decluttering - Intentional Choices for a Joyful Space

In the journey towards a clutter-free life, mindful decluttering plays a pivotal role. It involves making intentional choices that align with your values and bring you joy. Embracing mindful decluttering means being conscious of each item in your space and its impact on your well-being. This process isn't just about removing physical objects; it's about curating a living environment that nurtures your spirit and uplifts your soul.

Mindful decluttering invites you to reflect on the purpose and significance of every possession. It encourages a shift from accumulation to appreciation, from quantity to quality. By incorporating mindfulness into your decluttering efforts, you can savor the journey of letting go and embrace the liberation it brings. As you practice mindful decluttering, you'll find yourself surrounded only by things that resonate deeply with your essence, allowing your home to radiate with positivity and harmony.

When engaging in mindful decluttering, take the time to connect with each item. Consider its origin, its value to you, and its potential to enhance your living space. Letting go of the unnecessary opens up space for what truly matters, creating an environment that fosters creativity, tranquility, and contentment. The intention behind these decisions infuses your space with energy that revitalizes and rejuvenates your being.

Embracing mindful decluttering also means honoring sustainability and ethical consumption. It involves reevaluating your purchasing habits and choosing items that align with your eco-conscious values. By doing so, you contribute to a healthier planet and pave the way for a more sustainable lifestyle. Every intentional choice you make not only impacts your immediate surroundings but also ripples out to create positive changes in the world.

Furthermore, mindful decluttering empowers you to distinguish between what holds true significance and what simply occupies space. Through this process, you become adept at recognizing the essence of joy and fulfillment, fostering an environment where every object serves a meaningful purpose. Your home becomes a sanctuary of authenticity and delight, reflecting the beauty of a life curated with mindful intention.

As you journey through the art of mindful decluttering, remember to extend grace to yourself. Celebrate the progress made and appreciate the transformative impact each intentional choice brings. With mindful decluttering, you are not merely reshaping your living space; you are nourishing your spirit, cultivating gratitude, and embracing the boundless potential for joy in every moment.

Creating a Clarity-Driven Environment

In the pursuit of decluttering and creating a life filled with joy and purpose, the concept of a clarity-driven environment is essential. A clarity-driven environment encompasses not just the physical space around you, but also the mental and emotional atmosphere within. It's about fostering an environment that supports your well-being, encourages positive energy, and cultivates a sense of harmony.

To begin creating a clarity-driven environment, it's crucial to start with the physical space. Decluttering and organizing your surroundings can significantly impact your mental clarity and overall outlook. When your living space is free from unnecessary items and distractions, it becomes a sanctuary for relaxation, creativity, and inspiration. Consider implementing minimalist design principles, incorporating natural elements, and surrounding yourself with items that hold genuine value and beauty. Embracing simplicity can lead to a profound sense of serenity and balance within your home.

Beyond the physical realm, nurturing a clarity-driven environment involves tending to your mental and emotional well-being. This entails practicing mindfulness, cultivating gratitude, and letting go of negativity. Incorporating daily rituals such as meditation, journaling, or engaging in uplifting activities can shift your focus towards positivity and self-awareness. Surround yourself with affirming messages, motivational quotes, and engaging in self-care practices to foster an uplifting atmosphere.

Establishing clear boundaries and priorities further contributes to a clarity-driven environment. Learning to say 'no' when necessary and setting realistic expectations for yourself allows you to maintain a sense of balance and prevents overwhelm. By prioritizing tasks and relationships that are aligned with your values and goals, you create a nurturing and supportive environment for personal growth and fulfillment.

Ultimately, creating a clarity-driven environment requires consistent effort and commitment. Recognize that the journey towards clarity is not about perfection, but about progress. As you embrace the process of decluttering your physical, mental, and emotional spaces, you pave the way for a transformative experience. By consciously curating an environment that supports clarity, you open the door to endless possibilities and a life filled with purpose and joy.

Reflect and Rejoice - Celebrating Small Wins

The journey of decluttering is a transformative experience, and along this path, it's essential to celebrate the small victories. As you reflect on the progress made in your decluttering journey, take a moment to embrace the positive changes that have emerged. Recognize the sense of accomplishment as you clear each space, whether it's a drawer, a shelf, or an entire room. By acknowledging these small wins, you are fueling your motivation to continue the decluttering process.

Each item disposed of, each area organized, and each mindset shift deserves recognition. Take a moment to revel in the newfound freedom that comes with letting go of unnecessary possessions. Whether it's donating items to those in need, recycling, or throwing away unusable items, each action contributes to a lighter, more joyful environment.

Embracing gratitude for the effort put into decluttering cultivates a positive mindset and encourages further progress. Express thankfulness for your commitment and resilience throughout this process. By extending gratitude to yourself, you reinforce the value of your efforts and the importance of self-care during this transformation.

Let the satisfaction of reclaiming your space wash over you, allowing positivity to infuse every corner of your home. Embrace a moment of quiet reflection, recognizing the impact of your hard work. This act of appreciation will energize and inspire you to persist in your quest for a clutter-free life.

In addition to reflecting, it's equally crucial to acknowledge the emotional and mental shift that accompanies decluttering. Celebrate the newfound clarity and serenity that permeate your surroundings. Revel in the peace that arises from surrounding yourself with only what truly matters and brings joy. Every step taken to create a tranquil haven warrants celebration - you are crafting a sanctuary that reflects your most cherished aspirations and desires.

As you rejoice in these small wins, remember that the process of decluttering is not just about physical belongings; it's a holistic journey toward a more fulfilling life. Savor the liberation from material burdens and revel in the heightened sense of freedom. By celebrating these small triumphs, you are nurturing a space filled with positivity, tranquility, and happiness, aligning with your vision of a clutter-free, blissful existence.

Chapter 2

The Decluttering Process – Room by Room

Welcome to Your Clutter-Free Journey

Embarking on your clutter-free journey is an exhilarating and empowering step towards creating a space that rejuvenates your mind, body, and soul. As you begin this transformative process, it's vital to approach it with a positive mindset, embracing the opportunity to craft a restful sanctuary in your bedroom. By doing so, you're not just decluttering physical items; you're also decluttering your mind and setting the stage for peaceful rejuvenation. Each decision to let go of unnecessary items and organize your belongings is a celebration of self-care and self-love. The act of decluttering empowers you to reclaim control over your space and create an environment that fosters tranquility and serenity. It's not just about tidying up; it's about curating a space that reflects your aspirations, priorities, and dreams. As you walk through this journey, keep in mind that you're not just removing things - you're bringing in positivity, balance, and harmony into your life. This clutter-free journey is an act of self-compassion and renewal, a commitment to nurturing yourself and your surroundings. By starting with a positive mindset, you are laying the foundation for a truly enriching experience that extends far beyond the physical realm. So, embrace this as an opportunity to infuse joy, peace, and purpose into your living environment. This is the beginning of a beautiful transformation, and you are worthy of every moment of it.

Creating a Restful Bedroom Sanctuary

Your bedroom is more than just a place to sleep; it's your personal sanctuary, a haven of peace and tranquility. As you embark on your decluttering journey, it's essential to start with this sacred space where you begin and end each day. Imagine walking into your bedroom and feeling an instant sense of calm and serenity. This section will guide you through the process of transforming your bedroom into a restful oasis.

Begin by clearing out any unnecessary items from your bedroom. Keep only what brings you joy and contributes to the serene ambiance you desire. Consider reevaluating your bedding, curtains, and decor to create a soothing, cohesive look that promotes relaxation. Introduce soft textures, calming colors, and comforting scents to enhance the peaceful atmosphere. Implementing storage solutions such as under-bed organizers and wall-mounted shelves can help maintain a clutter-free, spacious feel in your bedroom.

Next, focus on organizing your clothing and personal belongings. Embrace the KonMari method or other decluttering techniques to assess each item's value and purpose. Curate a wardrobe that reflects your style and simplifies your daily routine. Devising a functional layout for your dressers, closets, and bedside tables can streamline your morning and evening rituals, minimizing stress and enhancing your overall well-being.

Incorporate elements of nature into your bedroom design, whether through potted plants, natural materials, or artwork inspired by the outdoors. The presence of greenery can evoke a sense of harmony and vitality, contributing to a rejuvenating ambiance. Illuminate your sanctuary with soft, ambient lighting to create a tranquil retreat conducive to rest and rejuvenation.

Finally, establish rejuvenating rituals to elevate your bedroom experience. Dedicate time for meditation, gentle stretching, or journaling to unwind before bedtime. Set the tone for peaceful slumber with a calming bedtime routine and create a designated area for gratitude practices or affirmations. By infusing your bedroom with positivity and intention, you can cultivate a space that nurtures your well-being and promotes restful nights.

As you witness your bedroom undergo this transformative process, revel in the newfound sense of tranquility and revitalization it brings. Your bedroom sanctuary should serve as a reminder of the endless possibilities that await as you continue your decluttering journey.

Living Room Harmony - Managing Common Spaces

Imagine stepping into your living room and feeling an immediate sense of peace and serenity. This is the power of creating living room harmony. Your living room is where family and friends gather, where laughter echoes and memories are made. It's a space that should radiate warmth and welcome, a sanctuary from the hustle and bustle of everyday life. Achieving living room harmony involves a delicate balance of decluttering and purposeful design. Start by assessing the layout to optimize flow and functionality. The key is to maintain a balance between comfort and minimalism, allowing space for movement while preserving the cozy atmosphere. Consider incorporating multi-functional furniture to maximize space and minimize clutter. Embrace natural light and strategically place plants to bring nature indoors, creating a calming ambiance. Personalize the space with meaningful décor that sparks joy and evokes positive emotions. By curating a space that reflects your personality and values, you infuse your living room with a sense of authenticity and harmony. Lastly, establish routines for maintaining order in this beloved space. Set aside a few minutes each day to tidy up and reset the room, ensuring that it remains a serene haven amidst the chaos of modern life. As you embrace the journey of managing your common spaces, relish in the transformative power of decluttering and intentional design. Your living room will become a source of rejuvenation, fostering deep connections and joyful moments for years to come.

Streamlining the Heart of the Home – The Kitchen

Embark on a journey of transformation as we delve into the heart of your home - the kitchen. This is more than just another decluttering task; it's an opportunity to revitalize this central space, where delectable creations come to life and fond memories are made. Begin by clearing all surfaces, opening up space for culinary adventures and fostering an airy ambiance that uplifts your spirits. Explore the contents of your cabinets and drawers with a discerning eye, ridding them of unused gadgets and chipped dinnerware to make room for items that truly resonate with your vision of a harmonious kitchen. Embrace the joy of organizing your pantry, arranging each staple and seasoning with care, creating a delightful and efficient system that simplifies meal preparations. Infuse personality into this sacred space by displaying cherished cookbooks or heirloom utensils, celebrating the artistry and love that goes into every dish. As you curate your kitchen environment, consider donating excess cookware or appliances to those in need, allowing your actions to spark joy beyond your own home. With newfound order and purpose, savor the delight of cooking and entertaining in a clutter-free kitchen, where every meal is imbued with nourishment for both body and soul. Let the revitalized energy of this space inspire and empower you to embrace a life filled with abundance and serenity.

Blissful Bathroom Transformation

The bathroom, a soothing oasis where you can wash away the day's stress and prepare for a new beginning. Transforming your bathroom into a blissful sanctuary is an essential step in creating a clutter-free and peaceful home. Begin by decluttering the countertops, removing expired products, and organizing items into accessible storage solutions. Consider adding elegant touches such as scented candles, plush towels, and lush plants to create a spa-like ambiance. Embrace a minimalist aesthetic by opting for sleek, functional storage units and eliminating unnecessary items. By curating a serene atmosphere, you can elevate your daily routine into a rejuvenating experience. Once the physical clutter is cleared, take a moment to assess the decor. Infuse the space with personal touches that bring joy, whether it's vibrant artwork, calming color schemes, or decorative accents. Artfully display your favorite items while keeping surfaces free from unnecessary objects, promoting a sense of calm and tranquility. Emphasize natural lighting and ventilation to enhance the feeling of openness and airiness, revitalizing the space and making it feel larger and more inviting. Thoughtfully chosen fixtures and thoughtful design elements could further elevate your bathroom, adding a touch of luxury to your daily rituals. From eco-friendly accessories to indulgent bath products, there are countless ways to transform this intimate space into a rejuvenating retreat. Finally, embrace a consistent cleaning routine to maintain your newly transformed bathroom. Cultivate a habit of regular tidying and cleaning to preserve the serenity and order you've created, ensuring that your sanctuary remains an uplifting haven. With these simple yet impactful adjustments, you can celebrate your personalized, blissful bathroom transformation—a pivotal expression of self-care and mindful living within your decluttered home.

Home Office Haven - Boosting Productivity

Designing a home office space that nurtures creativity and enhances productivity is an exhilarating endeavor. As you embark on this journey, envision a workspace filled with light, energy, and inspiration. Start by decluttering the area, allowing breathing room for innovation to flourish. Select furniture and decor that not only complements your style but also promotes comfort and efficiency. Utilize natural light and incorporate plants or artwork to infuse the space with vibrancy and positivity. Consider integrating ergonomic elements, such as an adjustable chair or a standing desk, to prioritize your physical well-being while working. Additionally, personalizing your workspace with meaningful trinkets or motivational quotes can serve as constant reminders of your purpose and goals. Organizing your office supplies and digital files in designated storage solutions will streamline your workflow and eliminate unnecessary stress. Create distinct zones for different tasks, whether it's a focused work area, a relaxation nook, or a brainstorming zone. Experiment with aromatherapy or soothing music to set the ambiance for ideal concentration and creativity. Furthermore, incorporating time management techniques, such as the Pomodoro method or task batching, can help structure your day and optimize productivity. Integrate breaks into your schedule to recharge and prevent burnout. Lastly, instill a sense of fulfillment in your daily routine by setting and celebrating achievable milestones. Cultivating a home office haven elevates your professional experience, as it becomes a sanctuary that fuels your passion and drive.

Garage and Storage Triumphs

Transforming your garage and storage spaces into organized, functional areas is a monumental step in your decluttering journey.

These often neglected spaces have the potential to become havens of order and efficiency. As you embark on this adventure, envision the garage as more than just a place for storing items. It can be a workshop, a home gym, or even a cozy corner for relaxation. Begin by clearing out items that no longer serve a purpose or bring you joy. Consider donating, selling, or recycling these items to free up valuable space and create a clean slate. Next, assess your storage needs and invest in shelving units, clear storage bins, and hooks to maximize vertical space. Utilize labels to easily identify the contents of each bin, eliminating the frustration of rummaging through endless boxes. Embrace the opportunity to customize the layout of your garage to suit your lifestyle. Create designated zones for gardening supplies, seasonal decorations, tools, and sports equipment, allowing for easy access and streamlined functionality. Make use of wall-mounted organizers for frequently used items such as bikes, rakes, and ladders, freeing up floor space and reducing clutter. As you witness your garage transform into an organized and accessible space, revel in the newfound sense of freedom and accomplishment. Celebrate your triumphs by sharing before-and-after photos with friends and family, inspiring them to embark on their own decluttering adventures. Revel in the joy of discovering forgotten treasures and reclaiming valuable square footage. With each item finding its rightful place, you are embracing a life filled with simplicity and intentionality. Your garage and storage spaces are not just containers for belongings; they are reflections of your commitment to living a clutter-free and purposeful life. Embrace this transformation with gratitude and enthusiasm, knowing that every step propels you closer to a harmonious and uplifting living environment.

Mastering Closet and Wardrobe Organization

Are you tired of staring at a chaotic mess every time you open your closet doors? It's time to transform this often-neglected space into a serene sanctuary for your wardrobe. When you declutter and organize your closet, you're not just creating physical order – you're making space for positive energy and self-care. Start by pulling everything out of your closet and assessing each item. As you sort through your clothes, ask yourself if each piece brings you joy or serves a purpose in your current life. Let go of anything that no longer resonates with who you are today. Once you've decluttered, it's time to organize. Consider investing in space-saving storage solutions like hanging organizers, clear storage bins, and shelf dividers. Group similar items together, such as pants, shirts, dresses, and accessories, so you can easily find what you need. Remember to make the most of vertical space by using stackable shelves or hanging shoe racks. As you arrange your clothing, think about creating a system that reflects your daily routine. Place frequently worn items at eye level and seasonal or occasional pieces on higher or lower shelves. Don't forget to leave some room for future additions to your wardrobe, and consider rotating seasonal items to keep your closet fresh and inspiring. Lastly, embrace the power of gratitude as you organize your closet. Acknowledge the abundance of choices you have and express appreciation for the clothes you're keeping. Each time you open your newly organized closet, feel a sense of pride and joy at the beautiful, clutter-free space you've created. Your revitalized closet will not only simplify your morning routine but also serve as a daily reminder of the positivity and self-care you've welcomed into your life.

Effortless Maintenance Tips for Each Room

Now that you have successfully decluttered and organized each room in your home, it's essential to incorporate effortless maintenance tips to ensure that your space remains clutter-free and harmonious. Let's delve into specific strategies for maintaining the serenity and order you've achieved.

Firstly, set a daily routine for tidying up. Spend a few minutes each day to put away items that have migrated from their designated spots. By making this a consistent practice, you'll prevent clutter from accumulating and maintain a sense of calm in your home.

In addition, designate a specific day each week for deeper cleaning and organization tasks. Carve out time to dust, vacuum, and perform any necessary upkeep in each room. This proactive approach will help you stay on top of maintaining your newly decluttered space and prevent the reemergence of chaos.

Furthermore, consider implementing the 'one in, one out' rule. Whenever you acquire a new item, make it a habit to remove an existing item to donate, recycle, or discard. Adhering to this principle ensures that your possessions remain in balance, preventing unnecessary accumulation and preserving the streamlined environment you've cultivated.

Another valuable strategy is to regularly assess your belongings and identify any items that no longer serve a purpose or bring joy. By conducting periodic mini-decluttering sessions, you can prevent unnecessary build-up and maintain a well-organized living space.

Moreover, embrace the power of labeling. Whether it's using clear storage containers or adding labels to drawers and bins, clear identification streamlines the process of finding and returning items to their designated homes, contributing to the overall maintenance of your organized spaces.

Lastly, celebrate your progress! Recognize and acknowledge the positive impact your decluttering efforts have had on your life. Take time to reflect on the transformation of your home, revel in the newfound sense of ease and fulfillment, and use this motivation to fuel your commitment to maintaining a clutter-free environment.

Incorporating these effortless maintenance tips into your daily life will ensure that the harmony and order you've achieved through decluttering persist, creating a peaceful and uplifting living environment for years to come.

Celebrating Your Progress - Reflect and Rejoice

After implementing the decluttering process room by room, it's time to celebrate your incredible progress. Take a moment to reflect on how far you've come in transforming your living space into a harmonious and clutter-free sanctuary. Embrace the sense of accomplishment and empowerment that comes with taking control of your environment. Each room holds unique memories of your journey, and it's essential to acknowledge the positive changes that have taken place. While reflecting on your achievements, allow yourself to feel grateful for the newfound sense of peace and clarity that accompanies a clutter-free home. The joy that comes from reclaiming your space is worth celebrating. Whether you started this journey to enhance your well-being, increase productivity, or simply to create a serene environment, take pride in the strides you have made. As you rejoice in the transformation of each room, consider the positive impact this has had on your overall mindset and daily life. Embrace the renewed energy and inspiration that now flow effortlessly through your rejuvenated living space. Share your success with others and inspire them to embark on their own decluttering journey. By celebrating your progress, you reinforce the positive habits and mindsets that have contributed to your success. This celebration is not just about the physical decluttering but also a reflection of your inner growth and determination. Use this opportunity to recognize the strength and resilience you possess as you continue to create a nurturing and inspiring environment. Finally, take a moment to envision the future you desire within your clutter-free space. Let this vision guide you as you maintain and further enhance the tranquil oasis you've cultivated. Continue to build on the momentum of your progress and carry forward the sense of fulfillment and contentment that accompanies a clutter-free lifestyle. With reflection and rejoicing, you reaffirm your commitment to a harmonious life, setting the stage for ongoing joy and peace within your home.

Chapter 3

Decluttering Beyond the Physical - Mind, Digital Space, and Relationships

Clearing the Mind - Techniques for Mental Declutter

In today's digital era, our minds often become cluttered with constant stimuli. Finding inner peace and mental clarity amidst the chaos may seem daunting, but fear not, for there are numerous empowering techniques at your disposal to achieve a tranquil state of mind.

Meditation stands as a pillar of mental decluttering, offering an oasis of tranquility in the midst of life's whirlwind. By practicing focused breathing and mindfulness, one can gently release the hold of racing thoughts and ground oneself in the present moment. The beauty of meditation lies in its accessibility—whether through guided sessions, apps, or simply quiet introspection, anyone can embark on this transformative journey toward mental serenity.

Another powerful avenue for clearing the mind is journaling—a sacred ritual that enables individuals to pour their innermost thoughts onto blank pages. Engaging in expressive writing not only untangles the web of emotions but also provides a tangible record of personal growth. Through the act of journaling, it becomes possible to gain invaluable insights into one's internal landscape, paving the way for healing and self-discovery.

The art of mindfulness plays a pivotal role in decluttering the mind, inviting individuals to anchor themselves in the present moment. By savoring simple sensory experiences and embracing gratitude, one can gently sweep away the clutter of worries and anxieties, fostering a sense of inner peace and appreciation for life's wondrous tapestry.

Incorporating these practices into your daily routine presents a gateway to mental rejuvenation, allowing you to shed burdens and nurture a harmonious balance within. Let these techniques be your guiding stars as you embark on a journey toward mental decluttering and empowerment.

Digital Harmony - Organizing Your Online Life

In today's digital age, our online presence plays a significant role in our daily lives. With the vast amount of information available at our fingertips, it's essential to create a harmonious and organized digital space that promotes productivity and positivity. Organizing your online life involves decluttering your digital environment, managing your digital assets efficiently, and cultivating a healthy relationship with technology. Start by decluttering your inbox and unsubscribing from unnecessary newsletters or promotional emails that add to the digital noise. Create folders and labels to categorize your emails for easy access and retrieval. As you organize your digital files, consider using cloud storage services to secure important documents and photos while reducing clutter on your devices. Embrace digital minimalism by evaluating your apps and digital subscriptions, keeping only those that serve a purpose or bring you joy. Streamline your social media accounts by unfollowing accounts that no longer align with your interests or values. Engage in meaningful interactions and curate your feed to inspire and uplift your online experience. Set boundaries for screen time and prioritize offline activities that promote real connections and well-being. Implement digital detox routines such as unplugging from devices during designated times to foster mindfulness and reduce digital overwhelm. Establish an inspiring digital sanctuary by customizing your device backgrounds with uplifting images or quotes that resonate with your aspirations. Embrace digital balance by leveraging technology to enhance your life without allowing it to consume your attention entirely. As you cultivate digital harmony, you'll create a nurturing online space that amplifies your well-being and supports your journey towards a clutter-free life.

Streamlining Schedules - Managing Time and Energy

In our journey to declutter beyond the physical, we arrive at the critical facet of managing time and energy – the very essence of our daily lives. The art of streamlining schedules encompasses a harmonious blend of efficiency and mindfulness. It's about optimizing every moment without succumbing to the pressures of a hectic pace. So, how do we embark on this enlightening path of balanced living? Start by embracing the power of prioritization. Identify the most impactful tasks that align with your goals and values. By directing your focus towards these priorities, you create a sense of purpose and fulfillment. This mindful approach empowers you to manage your time and energy intentionally, giving precedence to what truly matters. As you embrace this mindset, remember the significance of balance. Cultivate rhythms in your day that allow for both productivity and rejuvenation. Establishing boundaries around your time ensures that you allocate sufficient moments for rest, relaxation, and personal growth. Embrace the concept of saying 'yes' to activities that nourish your soul and 'no' to those that drain your energy. By doing so, you honor your well-being and preserve your vitality. Furthermore, consider the value of delegation and automation. Identify tasks that can be entrusted to others or systems, enabling you to invest your energy where it is most needed. Alongside this, learn to let go of perfectionism and embrace progress. Celebrate small victories, and recognize that imperfection is part of the human experience. Lastly, in your quest for streamlined schedules, infuse positivity and gratitude into your daily rituals. Cultivate a mindset of abundance, celebrating the present and looking forward to the future with optimism. As you navigate through life with greater ease and intention, remember that managing time and energy is not solely about productivity – it's about creating space for joy, connection, and personal growth. Ultimately, by streamlining your life's rhythm, you pave the way for a more fulfilling and uplifting existence.

Healthy Connections - Evaluating Relationships

Building and nurturing meaningful relationships is a vital aspect of leading a fulfilling life. When embarking on the journey of decluttering beyond the physical, it's crucial to acknowledge the significance of our connections with others. Evaluating relationships allows us to foster environments that cultivate positivity and growth. It begins with recognizing the impact individuals have on our mental and emotional well-being, and vice versa. By assessing and refining our connections, we create space for healthy, supportive interactions that align with our values and aspirations.

The first step in evaluating relationships involves reflecting on the dynamics at play. Take note of how various relationships make you feel. Are they uplifting, encouraging, and empowering, or do they drain your energy and bring negativity into your life? Identifying these patterns can offer valuable insights into which relationships contribute positively to your growth and which ones may require boundaries or reevaluation.

Next, it's essential to communicate openly and honestly with those in your circle. Express your appreciation for the positive influences and discuss any concerns or challenges that may arise. Healthy communication lays the foundation for understanding and empathy, fostering stronger, more authentic connections. Furthermore, setting boundaries ensures that your relationships align with your intentions and values while creating a sense of balance and harmony in your interactions.

As you evaluate your relationships, prioritize spending time with individuals who lift you up and share your enthusiasm for personal development. Surrounding yourself with supportive, like-minded individuals cultivates an environment conducive to growth and positivity. Additionally, be mindful of the energy you bring into your relationships, offering support and encouragement to others as well.

Embracing a decluttered approach to relationships doesn't necessarily mean cutting ties altogether. It may involve reprioritizing certain connections, establishing clear boundaries, or seeking understanding and growth together. Ultimately, the goal is to surround yourself with individuals who enrich your life and inspire you to be the best version of yourself. By evaluating and evolving our relationships, we embark on a journey of personal empowerment and alignment with the uplifting connections that contribute to our well-being.

Mindful Consumption - Being Selective About Inputs

In our journey to declutter our lives, it's essential to recognize the impact of our daily consumption. Mindful consumption means being selective about the information, media, and material possessions that we allow into our lives. When we actively choose to surround ourselves with positivity, inspiration, and knowledge, we pave the way for a more fulfilling existence. It's about fostering an environment that nurtures our personal growth and happiness.

One aspect of mindful consumption involves evaluating the media we expose ourselves to. Whether it's the news, social media, or entertainment, being aware of how these inputs affect our mental state is crucial. We can curate our media intake by opting for content that uplifts, educates, and motivates us. By doing so, we create a mental landscape that promotes optimism and resilience.

Material consumption also plays a significant role in decluttering our lives. Adopting a mindful approach to acquiring possessions allows us to focus on quality over quantity. It encourages us to invest in items that serve a purpose or bring genuine joy, steering us away from impulsive or excessive buying. This shift in mindset not only reduces clutter in our physical space but also cultivates a sense of appreciation for the things that truly enrich our lives.

Furthermore, being discerning about the information we absorb empowers us to shape our perspectives and beliefs consciously. By seeking out knowledge that expands our understanding of the world, we embrace personal growth and open ourselves up to new possibilities. It's about actively pursuing wisdom and insights that align with our values and aspirations, propelling us toward a more purposeful existence.

Embracing mindful consumption doesn't mean depriving ourselves of enjoyment; rather, it encourages us to savor meaningful experiences. Whether it's savoring a well-curated book, relishing deep conversations, or immersing ourselves in nature's beauty, this intentional approach ensures that we derive true fulfillment from the moments we cherish.

Ultimately, by practicing mindful consumption, we take control of the inputs that shape our lives. We create an empowering ecosystem that fuels our passions, nurtures our well-being, and harmonizes our inner and outer worlds. With each deliberate choice, we embark on a transformative journey toward a life abundant with purpose, meaning, and joy.

Creating Boundaries - Protecting Your Time and Space

Setting boundaries is a powerful act of self-care. By clearly defining what is acceptable and what is not in your life, you can protect your precious time and space from unnecessary clutter and stress. This involves learning to say no to things that do not align with your priorities and values, and saying yes to opportunities that bring joy and fulfillment.While it may initially feel daunting to establish boundaries, it ultimately empowers you to create a life that is in harmony with your true desires and aspirations. When you respect your own time and space, others are more likely to do the same, fostering healthier and more meaningful relationships. Protecting your time and space requires clear communication, assertiveness, and self-awareness. It involves recognizing when to step back and recharge, and when to engage and contribute. It means acknowledging that your mental and physical well-being are non-negotiable, and honoring the commitments and activities that truly resonate with you. By doing so, you cultivate an environment that supports your personal growth and nourishes your spirit. As you embrace this practice, you'll find yourself experiencing a greater sense of freedom and fulfillment. Remember, creating boundaries is not about building walls; it's about constructing bridges that connect you to what truly matters. It's about cultivating an environment that uplifts and energizes you, allowing you to pursue your passions and dreams with clarity and purpose.

Nurturing Emotional Health - Sustaining Mental Clarity

In the pursuit of a clutter-free life, it's essential to acknowledge the profound impact that emotional well-being has on our ability to maintain mental clarity. Nurturing emotional health is not merely an aspect of decluttering; it is a cornerstone for sustaining a joyful and purposeful existence. By fostering emotional resilience, individuals can navigate the inevitable ups and downs of life with grace and fortitude. Embracing positivity and gratitude forms the bedrock upon which a healthy emotional landscape is built. Through daily practices of mindfulness, self-compassion, and empathy, individuals can cultivate an environment where emotional balance thrives. Being attuned to one's feelings while also learning to constructively process and release negative emotions is crucial in this journey. It's a continuous exercise in self-love and understanding, allowing individuals to face challenges with optimism and a resilient spirit. Engaging in activities that bring joy and fulfillment, such as hobbies, creative endeavors, and spending quality time with loved ones, significantly contributes to emotional nourishment. Creating space for moments of self-care, whether through meditation, journaling, or relaxation techniques, further reinforces emotional well-being. Cultivating authentic connections and meaningful relationships plays a pivotal role in nurturing emotional health. Surrounding oneself with compassionate, supportive individuals fosters a sense of belonging and uplifts the spirit during difficult times. Actively seeking out opportunities to provide acts of kindness and support also enriches one's emotional landscape, creating a reciprocal cycle of positivity. Recognizing the importance of emotional wellness in the quest for a clutter-free life empowers individuals to confront challenges and setbacks with a clear mind and resilient heart. It is a holistic approach that encompasses not only decluttering physical spaces but also creating an environment that nurtures emotional harmony. By sustaining mental clarity through a foundation of emotional well-being, individuals are better equipped to embrace the beauty of simplicity and lead a purpose-driven life.

Balancing Priorities - Simplifying Daily Decisions

In our journey to declutter beyond the physical realm, we encounter the pivotal aspect of balancing priorities in order to simplify our daily decisions. Life presents us with a multitude of choices every day, from the moment we wake up to the time we finally lay our heads down to rest. This abundance of options can often lead to decision fatigue, causing us to feel overwhelmed and drained. However, by consciously aligning our priorities, we can alleviate much of this stress.

The first step in balancing priorities is to identify what truly matters to us. By taking the time to reflect on our values and aspirations, we gain clarity on the aspects of life that hold the most significance for us. This awareness empowers us to make decisions that are aligned with our priorities, ultimately leading to a more fulfilling and purpose-driven existence.

Upon recognizing our priorities, we can then begin to streamline our daily activities. By categorizing tasks and responsibilities based on their importance and impact, we can create a clear roadmap for our day. This organized approach not only saves time and effort but also allows us to focus on what truly matters, fostering a sense of accomplishment and satisfaction.

Another fundamental aspect of balancing priorities is the art of saying no. Often, we find ourselves entangled in commitments and obligations that do not serve our best interests or align with our goals. Learning to graciously decline such distractions enables us to channel our energy into endeavors that resonate with our priorities, nurturing both our personal growth and well-being.

Moreover, maintaining a balanced perspective plays a crucial role in simplifying daily decisions. By acknowledging that not every task or request demands immediate attention, we can avoid spreading ourselves too thin and preserve our mental and emotional resources for endeavors that truly reflect our priorities.

As we embrace the practice of balancing priorities, we experience a profound shift in our daily experiences. The seemingly daunting array of choices transforms into opportunities for intentional living and fulfillment. Each decision becomes a reflection of our values, propelling us closer to our aspirations and deepening our connection with our true selves. Ultimately, through the simple yet profound act of aligning our daily choices with our priorities, we pave the way for a life brimming with purpose, joy, and inner contentment.

Embracing Minimalism - Less is More

Minimalism is not simply a design aesthetic; it's a way of life that promotes living with intention and purpose. Embracing minimalism allows individuals to focus on what truly matters, stripping away the excess to reveal the essence of life. By consciously choosing to simplify, one can experience a sense of freedom and clarity that transcends material possessions. In a cluttered world filled with distractions, embracing minimalism offers a refreshing perspective.

At its core, minimalism encourages individuals to assess their belongings and commitments, evaluating each in terms of necessity and value. This process fosters mindfulness, enabling individuals to let go of the unnecessary and embrace the essential. It's about quality over quantity, emphasizing experiences and relationships over material possessions. By embracing minimalism, individuals can gain more control over their lives, aligning their actions with their values and priorities.

In a society that often equates success with accumulation, embracing minimalism challenges the notion that more is always better. It celebrates the beauty of simplicity, teaching individuals to find contentment in what they already have rather than constantly seeking more. Through this shift in mindset, individuals can cultivate gratitude and develop a deeper appreciation for the present moment. Minimalism empowers individuals to declutter not only their physical spaces but also their mental and emotional landscapes.

Beyond the tangible benefits, embracing minimalism can lead to a sustainable and environmentally conscious lifestyle. By consuming less and repurposing what we already possess, we contribute to reducing waste and minimizing our ecological footprint. As we simplify our lives, we also reduce our impact on the planet, promoting a harmonious coexistence with the natural world.

Embracing minimalism is an ongoing journey, not a destination. It's about continuously reassessing and refining our priorities, letting go of what no longer serves us, and embracing the beauty of living with less. The rewards of embracing minimalism are abundant—mental clarity, reduced stress, enhanced creativity, and a renewed sense of purpose. By recognizing that less is indeed more, individuals can create space for what truly matters, allowing joy, gratitude, and fulfillment to flourish.

Living Harmoniously - Integrating a Clutter-Free Lifestyle

Living harmoniously in a clutter-free lifestyle is not just about maintaining order in our physical surroundings; it's about cultivating a mindset that values simplicity, embraces joy, and encourages mindfulness in all aspects of our lives. As we continue on this journey of decluttering and minimalism, it's important to remember that the ultimate goal is not just an organized home, but a balanced and fulfilling life. To truly integrate a clutter-free lifestyle, we must extend the principles of minimalism beyond material possessions and into our daily routines, relationships, and overall well-being.

One of the key foundations for living harmoniously in a clutter-free lifestyle is gratitude. By cultivating an attitude of gratitude, we can shift our focus from what we lack to appreciating what we already have. This shift in perspective enables us to find contentment in simplicity and reduces the desire for excessive accumulation. Practicing gratitude allows us to see the beauty in the little things and brings a sense of abundance into our lives, enriching our experiences and relationships.

Another essential aspect of integrating a clutter-free lifestyle is mindful consumption. Being intentional about what we bring into our lives, whether it's material goods, information, or commitments, empowers us to make conscious choices that align with our values and goals. By adopting a discerning approach to consumption, we can avoid the cycle of mindless accumulation and instead surround ourselves only with possessions and experiences that truly enhance our lives. Mindful consumption also extends to our digital spaces, encouraging us to curate our online environment and minimize digital distractions, thus fostering mental clarity and focus.

As we strive to live harmoniously in a clutter-free lifestyle, it becomes crucial to prioritize self-care and holistic wellness. Simplifying our schedules and de-cluttering our commitments allows us to create space for activities that nurture our physical, emotional, and spiritual well-being. Engaging in mindfulness practices, regular exercise, adequate rest, and meaningful connections cultivates a balanced and harmonious lifestyle. By prioritizing self-care, we fortify our resilience, boost our productivity, and foster a deep sense of fulfillment. Additionally, integrating moments of stillness and reflection into our daily routine provides opportunities for self-discovery and personal growth, contributing to a more meaningful and purposeful existence.

Ultimately, embracing and integrating a clutter-free lifestyle is a transformative journey that encompasses more than just organization and tidiness. It is a mindset shift towards intentional living, where we prioritize what truly matters and let go of what no longer serves us. By embracing gratitude, practicing mindful consumption, and prioritizing holistic wellness, we create a life imbued with ease, intentionality, and joy. Living harmoniously in a clutter-free lifestyle opens the door to a world of abundance, allowing us to savor the present moment and design a future filled with meaning and fulfillment.

Chapter 4

The 30-Day Decluttering Challenge - Week by Week

Intro to Your 30-Day Journey

What an exciting adventure you're embarking on! The next 30 days are going to be a transformative journey for you and your living space. As you delve into the 30-day decluttering challenge, you're not just tidying up your physical surroundings - you're creating space for positivity, abundance, and joy to flow into your life. This challenge is designed to help you break free from the constraints of clutter, allowing you to rediscover the beauty and potential of your home. By committing to this challenge, you're making a powerful statement to yourself – that you deserve a living environment that uplifts and energizes you every single day. Throughout the weeks ahead, you'll witness the remarkable impact of your efforts unfold. Each decluttering decision you make will pave the way for greater clarity, productivity, and peace within your living spaces. As you free yourself from unnecessary possessions and emotional baggage, you'll experience a profound sense of liberation and empowerment. Not only will your physical environment undergo a remarkable transformation, but you'll also notice a significant shift in your mental and emotional well-being. The benefits of this 30-day journey extend far beyond just a tidy home. You'll find yourself feeling lighter, more focused, and ready to embrace new opportunities with renewed vitality. Together, we'll explore practical strategies, motivational insights, and mutual support as we navigate this enriching experience. Remember, this isn't just about decluttering – it's about reshaping your lifestyle and reclaiming control over your environment. So, stay committed and enthusiastic, and get ready to unlock a world of possibilities as we embark on this 30-day decluttering challenge.

Week 1: Jumpstart Your Success - Setting the Stage

Congratulations! You've taken the first step towards transforming your living space and, subsequently, your life. Week 1 is all about setting the stage for an exhilarating journey towards a clutter-free existence. It's a time for embracing newfound perspectives and igniting the spark of motivation within you. As you embark on this week, visualize the vibrant, uncluttered surroundings that await you. Take a moment to appreciate the potential and possibilities that lie beneath the layers of disarray. Designate a specific area in your home as the starting point of your decluttering expedition.

Begin with one small, manageable space to build positive momentum. Set the intention to create a haven that radiates tranquility and positivity. Embrace the process with unwavering determination and a sense of joyful anticipation. Remember, every item discarded brings you closer to an invigorating sense of liberation and clarity. Savor the satisfaction of each bag filled for donation or discard. Seek inspiration from the positive changes taking place around you and within you. Engage in gentle self-reflection to recognize the emotional attachments that may be hindering your decluttering progress. Cultivate resilience and optimism by acknowledging that this journey is a celebration of your commitment to personal growth. Encourage yourself with affirmations and visualize the delightful, clutter-free spaces awaiting you. Surround yourself with supportive individuals who champion your aspirations and share in your joy of transformation. Take this opportunity to foster mutual encouragement and exchange creative decluttering ideas. Inevitably, this initial phase is accompanied by moments of self-discovery and empowerment. It's an opportunity to reclaim your sense of agency over your living environment. Stay attuned to the transformative power of this endeavor, nurturing a mindset of abundance and gratitude. This week is the cornerstone of a truly magical journey towards a life liberated from the weight of clutter. Revel in the vibrant energy and renewed purpose that accompanies this wondrous beginning.

Week 2: High-Impact Targets - Making a Big Difference Fast

In this pivotal second week of your decluttering challenge, you're geared up to make substantial strides toward a clutter-free haven. As you dive into Week 2, empower yourself with the understanding that your efforts are about to yield remarkable results. This week, we focus on identifying and addressing high-impact targets – areas or items that, once decluttered, will immediately elevate your living environment. Embrace the exhilarating notion that by tackling these key spaces or possessions, you're not only streamlining your surroundings but also creating space for joy and relaxation. Throughout the week, revel in the sense of empowerment that comes with taking charge of your environment and transforming it into a sanctuary. Each day presents an opportunity to make discernible progress, reinforcing the unparalleled satisfaction that accompanies purposeful decluttering. By honing in on high-impact targets, you're fast-tracking your journey to a revitalized and uplifting living space. The positive energy you generate through intentional decluttering becomes palpable, infusing your home with newfound vibrancy and serenity. Stay fueled by the vision of your beautifully curated haven as you navigate Week 2, embracing the invigorating potential of each decisive action. Are you ready to witness the stunning transformation that awaits when you unleash your determination and focus on these high-impact targets? Prepare to be amazed by the profound impact of your dedicated efforts as you soar through this enriching week, propelling yourself closer to the liberating prospect of a clutter-free paradise.

Week 3: Uncovering Hidden Gems - Tackling the Often Overlooked

In Week 3 of your decluttering challenge, we embark on an exhilarating journey of uncovering hidden gems within your living space. This week is dedicated to addressing the often overlooked areas that hold immense potential for positive transformation. One of the key principles here is to embrace the concept of 'less is more,' recognizing the beauty and functionality of a streamlined environment. We begin by delving into those storage areas that tend to accumulate miscellaneous items over time. Whether it's the attic, basement, or closets, these spaces hold the promise of revealing forgotten treasures and releasing unnecessary burdens. As you start sorting through these areas, envision the liberation that comes with letting go of items that no longer serve a purpose or bring joy. Alongside physical spaces, we also take a deep dive into digital clutter. This could include tackling overflowing email inboxes, organizing digital files, and decluttering your virtual workspace. Uncovering hidden gems extends beyond material possessions and digital spaces; it also involves nurturing neglected aspects of our lives, such as self-care, hobbies, and relationships.

Week 3 encourages you to allocate time for activities that may have been sidelined by clutter and chaos. This could involve carving out space for mindfulness practices, reconnecting with old hobbies, or fostering meaningful connections with loved ones. By doing so, you'll unearth the intrinsic value of these often overlooked facets, bringing a renewed sense of joy and fulfillment into your life. The key to success in Week 3 lies in maintaining a positive mindset and celebrating every small victory along the way. Take pride in the progress you make, no matter how incremental it may seem, and allow each step forward to inspire and motivate you. Remember, the act of decluttering goes beyond creating physical space – it's about creating mental clarity, emotional harmony, and a rejuvenated spirit. As you embark on this transformative journey during Week 3, cherish the process and cultivate gratitude for the newfound treasures you uncover – both within your surroundings and within yourself.

Week 4: The Home Stretch - Bringing It All Together

As we enter Week 4 of your decluttering journey, you have already made remarkable progress in transforming your living space and your mindset. This week is all about celebrating your achievements and bringing everything together for a lasting impact. It's time to wrap up this transformative experience with a sense of accomplishment and empowerment.

During this week, focus on the areas that might still need a bit of attention. Look around your living spaces and identify any remaining items that could benefit from a new home or a chance to shine once again. Embrace the process with enthusiasm, knowing that every step you take brings you closer to your vision of an organized, serene environment.

Emphasize the importance of creating designated spaces for everything in your home. Whether it's a dedicated bin for shoes by the entryway or labeled containers for craft supplies, ensuring that each item has its own place will maintain the tidy, clutter-free atmosphere you've worked so hard to cultivate. Remember, an organized home leads to an organized mind.

As you approach the end of this amazing journey, take a moment to reflect on the personal growth and newfound clarity you've experienced. Acknowledge the positive impact decluttering has had on your overall well-being and continue to visualize the joyful, uncluttered life that lies ahead. Each decision to let go of unnecessary items paves the way for a brighter, more uplifting future.

Celebrate the achievements of this past month and acknowledge the effort and dedication you've put into this life-changing process.

By taking the time to appreciate your progress, you'll instill a deep sense of pride and motivation to continue maintaining your newly organized space. As you complete the final week of the decluttering challenge, remember that this is just the beginning of a fulfilling journey toward a harmonious, clutter-free lifestyle.

Daily Delight - Your Daily Decluttering Checklist

Imagine waking up each day to a serene and organized living space, where every item has its place and your mind feels uncluttered. This can be your reality with the daily delight of following a decluttering checklist. Each day, as you embark on this journey, remind yourself that you are taking intentional steps towards creating a harmonious environment for yourself.

To kickstart your day on a positive note, begin by making your bed. It may seem like a small task, but it sets the tone for the rest of the day and gives you a sense of accomplishment right from the start. As you move through your home, take a few minutes to return items to their designated spots. Whether it's hanging up clothes or putting away dishes, these little acts of tidying keep the clutter at bay.

Incorporate moments of mindfulness into your routine. Take a few minutes to appreciate the beauty in your surroundings and express gratitude for the progress you've made. By nurturing a grateful mindset, you'll find renewed energy to tackle any remaining areas of disarray.

Throughout the day, set aside a few moments for targeted decluttering tasks. Perhaps it's clearing out a junk drawer or organizing a shelf. These small victories add up and contribute to your overall sense of order and tranquility.

As evening approaches, take inventory of your accomplishments and revel in the satisfaction of a well-spent day. Reflect on how the concerted effort you put into decluttering is manifesting positive changes in your life. Reward yourself for staying committed to this transformative journey, knowing that each day you're one step closer to your ideal living environment.

End your day by preparing for tomorrow. Set out anything that needs to be addressed the following day and take a moment to visualize the peaceful, clutter-free space you aim to wake up to. You've invested in yourself and your well-being, and this consistent effort will continue to blossom into a meaningful and fulfilling lifestyle.

Sustaining Momentum - Tips to Stay Inspired and Engaged

Maintaining momentum during a 30-day decluttering challenge is essential for long-term success. As you progress through the weeks, it's natural to encounter moments of fatigue or doubt, but fear not! There are numerous strategies to help keep you inspired and engaged throughout your journey.

First and foremost, celebrate each small victory along the way. Recognizing the progress you've made, no matter how minor it may seem, can be incredibly motivating. Take a moment to appreciate the newly organized space or the possessions you've decided to let go of. By doing so, you're reinforcing the positive impact of decluttering in your life.

Another effective technique is to visualize the end result. Envision the tranquil, clutter-free environment you're working towards. Remind yourself of the mental and emotional benefits that await you once the process is complete. This mental image can serve as a powerful source of motivation during challenging moments.

Furthermore, consider involving friends or family members in your decluttering journey. Sharing your experiences with others not only provides accountability but also fosters a sense of camaraderie and support. Collaborating with loved ones can make the process more enjoyable and enhance your commitment to the challenge.

To maintain enthusiasm, vary your approach to decluttering. Embrace creativity by incorporating fun and innovative methods into your organization efforts. Whether it's rearranging furniture, experimenting with new storage solutions, or repurposing items, injecting novelty into the process can reignite your passion for decluttering.

Lastly, feed your inspiration by exposing yourself to uplifting decluttering stories and resources. Seek out books, articles, or online communities dedicated to decluttering success stories. Immerse yourself in the experiences of others who have transformed their lives through decluttering. Their journeys can serve as beacons of hope and fortitude, reminding you that you're not alone in your quest for a clutter-free existence.

By implementing these tips and embracing the supportive energy around you, you'll cultivate a resilient spirit that propels you forward, ensuring that you stay consistently engaged and inspired throughout the 30-day decluttering challenge.

Turning Challenges into Triumphs - Staying Committed

When embarking on your decluttering journey, it's important to recognize that challenges may arise along the way. However, these challenges are nothing more than opportunities for triumph and growth. Staying committed to the process, despite inevitable obstacles, is key to achieving lasting success. One of the most powerful techniques for conquering challenges is to shift your mindset from viewing them as roadblocks to seeing them as stepping stones. Embrace the hurdles as chances to learn, adapt, and ultimately emerge stronger. Recognize that setbacks are normal and part of the journey towards a clutter-free life. Develop resilience by shifting your focus from the challenges themselves to the lessons and strength gained from overcoming them. Stay committed to your vision of a harmonious, clutter-free space, and remember that every small victory brings you closer to your goal. Surround yourself with positivity and like-minded individuals who can offer support and encouragement during tough times. Share your challenges openly, seek advice, and celebrate each milestone achieved. By acknowledging and embracing challenges as integral parts of the journey towards decluttering success, you'll not only maintain your commitment but also thrive in the face of adversity. Remember, the path to a clutter-free life is paved with determination, courage, and unwavering commitment. Your triumph over challenges will not only transform your physical space but also strengthen your character and resilience in profound ways. Stay committed, stay focused, and witness how challenges become the fuel that propels you toward an uplifting and clutter-free lifestyle.

Real-Life Transformations - Success Stories to Inspire You

Lisa, a busy working mother, had always felt overwhelmed by the constant clutter in her home. She decided to take on the 30-Day Decluttering Challenge and, with each passing week, she noticed remarkable changes. With a small daily commitment, she transformed her home into a serene space where she could relax and enjoy quality time with her family.

Then there's Tom, a recent retiree who found the prospect of decluttering daunting at first. However, as he tackled one area at a time, he experienced a newfound sense of freedom and energy. Clearing out the physical clutter allowed him to declutter his mind and rediscover passions he had long neglected.

Joanna, a young professional, saw immense benefits from the challenge not only in her living space but also in her mental clarity and productivity. As she reclaimed her space, she found herself more inspired and motivated in her career, leading to new opportunities and growth.

These real-life success stories exemplify the transformative power of decluttering. They demonstrate that the journey to a clutter-free life is not just about organizing possessions, but about unlocking a renewed sense of joy, purpose, and fulfillment. When you commit to the process, as these individuals did, you open doors to new possibilities and experiences. Your clutter-free life awaits, filled with endless opportunities for growth and happiness.

Celebrating Your Achievements - Embrace Your Clutter-Free Life

The final stage of your 30-day decluttering challenge is a time for jubilation and reflection. As you stand in your transformed space, take a moment to appreciate the hard work, dedication, and commitment that brought you here. Your clutter-free life is not just an accomplishment; it's a testament to your resilience and determination.

Embrace this new chapter with gratitude and positivity. Celebrate each area of your home that has been liberated from clutter. Whether it's your organized closet, tidy kitchen, or streamlined workspace, every corner signifies a triumph over chaos. This celebration isn't just about material possessions; it's about reclaiming your peace of mind and creating an environment that nurtures your well-being.

As you revel in the serenity of your revitalized surroundings, take pride in the positive changes that have taken place within you during this journey. Recognize the strength and discipline you've cultivated as you confronted and conquered clutter. This is not solely a physical transformation but a profound emotional and mental shift towards a more harmonious way of living.

Share your success with those who have supported and cheered you on throughout this process. Whether it's family, friends, or online communities, allow yourself to bask in their acknowledgment and encouragement. Your achievement serves as inspiration, illustrating the potential for transformation and renewal in the lives of others. By celebrating together, you magnify the joy and significance of this monumental milestone.

Use this moment to reaffirm your commitment to maintaining your clutter-free lifestyle. Reflect on the invaluable lessons and newfound perspectives gained throughout the 30 days. Understand that this is not an endpoint but the beginning of an enduring journey towards simplicity and mindfulness. Let this celebration propel you forward, serving as a reminder of the profound impact of decluttering on your life.

Embrace your decluttered home as a sanctuary, a space that mirrors your aspirations and nurtures your dreams. Let it be a constant source of inspiration and tranquility. Most importantly, allow it to be a tangible representation of your unwavering belief in the power of transformative change. Remember, this celebration isn't just about the past 30 days; it's about embracing the limitless possibilities of a clutter-free life ahead.

Chapter 5

Maintaining a Clutter-Free Life – Habits and Mindsets for the Long Term

Embracing Daily Habits for Lasting Tidiness

Creating a harmonious and organized living environment is not just about large-scale decluttering efforts, but also about incorporating simple daily habits that promote tidiness and simplicity. By proactively embracing these habits, you can seamlessly integrate decluttering into your daily routine, ensuring lasting tidiness and an uncluttered living space.

Start by setting aside a few minutes each day to maintain order in your surroundings. Simple actions such as making your bed as soon as you wake up, putting items back in their designated places, and clearing countertops of unnecessary items can make a significant difference. Embrace the concept of 'do it now,' which encourages handling tasks immediately rather than allowing clutter to accumulate. This proactive mindset fosters a sense of control and efficiency in managing your living space.

In addition to daily tidying, consider incorporating mindful consumption practices into your life. Before purchasing new items, ask yourself if they truly add value or joy to your life. By being intentional with your belongings, you prevent unnecessary accumulation and promote a more minimalistic approach to living. As part of this process, regularly assess your possessions and let go of items that no longer serve a purpose or bring you happiness. Scheduling periodic donation or recycling sessions not only aids in decluttering but also in contributing to a more sustainable and environmentally conscious lifestyle.

Furthermore, cultivate a habit of gratitude for the things you already have. Appreciating the belongings that surround you can instill a sense of contentment and reduce the urge to continually acquire more possessions. Expressing gratitude for the functionality and beauty of your existing items reinforces a positive relationship with your living space, encouraging a less cluttered and more fulfilling environment.

As you integrate these simple yet powerful daily habits into your life, you will find that maintaining a clutter-free living space becomes effortless and natural. Each small act of tidying and intentional consumption aligns with your overarching goal of long-term tidiness, nurturing a space that reflects your values and brings tranquility to your everyday life.

Shifting Your Mindset for Continued Simplicity

In order to truly embrace a clutter-free life, it's essential to shift your mindset towards continued simplicity. This is more than just maintaining a tidy space; it's about fostering an attitude of appreciation for the simplicity and freedom that comes with de-cluttering. By cultivating a positive mindset, you can sustain your journey towards minimalism and create lasting change in your life.

One powerful mindset shift is realizing that less is more. Embracing this philosophy allows you to focus on what truly matters in life, rather than being weighed down by material possessions. It opens up space for creativity, gratitude, and meaningful experiences. As you adopt this mindset, you'll start to see the beauty in simplicity and find joy in the things that truly bring value to your life.

Another important shift in mindset involves letting go of attachment to belongings. Instead of clinging to items out of fear or nostalgia, embrace a mindset of abundance and trust in the future.

Understand that by releasing what no longer serves you, you make room for new opportunities, experiences, and relationships to enter your life. With this liberating perspective, decluttering becomes a freeing process rather than a daunting task.

Furthermore, adjusting your mindset involves reframing your relationship with consumerism. Rather than seeking fulfillment through constant consumption, cultivate a mentality of intentional living. When you shift your focus from acquiring more to cherishing what you already have, you'll find contentment within yourself and reduce the desire for unnecessary possessions. This shift can lead to a newfound sense of empowerment and purpose in living a clutter-free life.

Moreover, embracing a growth mindset is vital for continual simplicity. View decluttering as an ongoing journey of self-improvement and personal development. Approach obstacles and setbacks as opportunities for learning and growth, rather than reasons to give up. By maintaining a positive outlook and being open to change, you'll build resilience and perseverance, ensuring that your clutter-free lifestyle endures.

As you integrate these mindset shifts into your life, you'll discover that simplicity is not just a physical state, but a state of mind. Embracing these transformative perspectives will empower you to maintain a clutter-free environment with ease and joy, and lead a more fulfilling and purposeful life.

Scheduling Regular Decluttering Sessions

Maintaining a clutter-free life is not as simple as decluttering once and forgetting about it. It requires periodic attention and consistent effort. Scheduling regular decluttering sessions is the key to ensuring that your environment stays organized and uplifting. By setting aside dedicated time at regular intervals, you can prevent clutter from accumulating and maintain a serene living space.

Begin by marking specific dates on your calendar for these sessions. Treat them with the same importance as any other commitment, and honor them as essential appointments with yourself. Whether it's a monthly deep clean or weekly touch-ups, find a frequency that suits your lifestyle and stick to it. Consider enlisting the support of family members or housemates to participate in these sessions, turning decluttering into a collective activity that strengthens bonds and creates a sense of shared responsibility for the home.

During these sessions, focus on one area at a time instead of overwhelming yourself with the entire household. Start small, perhaps with a single drawer or a small section of a room, and systematically work through different areas over time. This approach ensures that decluttering never feels daunting and allows you to appreciate the progress made in each session. Celebrate every achievement, no matter how small, as it contributes to the overall tranquility of your surroundings.

As you establish this routine, observe how your mindset begins to shift. You may find that the act of decluttering becomes not just a chore, but a refreshing and rejuvenating experience. It becomes an opportunity to reconnect with your belongings, evaluate what truly adds value to your life, and release what no longer serves you. Over time, the practice of scheduling regular decluttering sessions instills a greater sense of control and mindfulness, nurturing a deeper connection with your living spaces.

By embracing these regular sessions, you set in motion a cycle of renewal and rejuvenation within your home. Each decluttering session becomes an act of self-care and respect for your environment, infusing your surroundings with positive energy and allowing your home to evolve alongside your personal growth. With dedication and commitment, the habit of scheduling regular decluttering sessions paves the way for lasting harmony and boundless joy within the spaces you cherish.

Adopting Minimalism for a Lifetime of Order

In the pursuit of a clutter-free life, adopting minimalism is an empowering and transformative choice. Embracing minimalism means consciously choosing to simplify your physical possessions, your mindset, and your overall lifestyle. It's about prioritizing what truly matters and letting go of the excess that weighs us down. Minimalism doesn't mean living with nothing; it means living with what brings you joy and purpose. By focusing on quality over quantity, you create a living environment that nurtures peace, clarity, and harmony. The minimalist philosophy extends beyond tangible belongings, emphasizing the value of experiences, relationships, and personal growth. This shift in perspective fosters a sense of liberation, freeing you from societal pressures and consumerism. As you adopt minimalism, you'll find yourself intentionally curating your surroundings, letting go of unnecessary distractions, and making space for what enriches your life. Through intentional choices, you'll cultivate a sense of abundance and fulfillment, realizing that true wealth lies in moments shared with loved ones, in pursuing passions, and in embracing the beauty of simplicity. Minimalism also encourages sustainability and mindful consumption, aligning with the preservation of our planet and leaving a positive impact on the world. As you integrate minimalism into your daily life, you'll notice a profound transformation taking place. Your home will become a sanctuary of tranquility, with each item serving a purpose and bringing joy. Your mind will embrace clarity and focus, no longer burdened by the weight of excess belongings. Your time and energy will be directed towards meaningful endeavors, allowing you to lead a purpose-driven life. Embracing minimalism isn't just a fleeting trend; it's a lifelong commitment to cultivating order and contentment. It's a conscious decision to surround yourself with items that reflect your values, aspirations, and identity. Through this deliberate curation, you empower yourself to live authentically, free from the constraints of materialism and comparison. With minimalism, you embark on a journey towards sustained simplicity and discover the profound beauty of living with intention. Ultimately, adopting minimalism paves the way for a life filled with clarity, gratitude, and boundless possibilities. It's a joyful invitation to prioritize what truly resonates with your soul, ensuring that every aspect of your existence aligns with your innermost desires and beliefs.

Overcoming Setbacks with Grace and Determination

Life is a series of ebbs and flows, and the journey towards maintaining a clutter-free life is no exception. While striving for a home and mind free from chaos can be incredibly rewarding, setbacks are an inevitable part of this process. It's crucial to approach these obstacles with grace and determination, viewing them not as failures, but as opportunities for growth and resilience. When faced with a setback, remember that it does not define your progress; rather, it serves as a chance to reaffirm your commitment to a clutter-free lifestyle.

One effective strategy for overcoming setbacks is to reframe challenges as learning experiences. Each stumbling block is an opportunity to reflect on what triggered the setback and how you can better navigate similar situations in the future. This shift in perspective empowers you to approach setbacks with curiosity and open-mindedness, fostering personal development along the way.

Furthermore, it's important to embrace self-compassion during times of difficulty. Instead of succumbing to self-criticism, extend kindness and understanding to yourself. Recognize that maintaining a clutter-free life is a continuous journey, and occasional setbacks do not overshadow the progress you have made. By practicing self-compassion, you cultivate a positive mindset that enables you to bounce back with renewed determination.

In addition, seek support from those who uplift and encourage you. Whether it's reaching out to friends, family members, or fellow decluttering enthusiasts, sharing your challenges with a supportive community can provide valuable perspective and motivation. Remember, you are not alone on this journey, and connecting with others who share similar aspirations can help you navigate setbacks with greater strength and resilience.

As you confront setbacks, stay mindful of your ultimate vision for a clutter-free life. Envision the peaceful and harmonious space you are striving to create, and let this vision reignite your passion and resolve. By focusing on the positive outcomes awaiting you, setbacks become mere detours rather than roadblocks, propelling you forward towards lasting transformation.

Finally, celebrate your triumphs, big and small, as you overcome setbacks. Acknowledge the resilience and determination that fuel your progress, and take pride in your ability to navigate challenges with grace. By embracing setbacks as integral components of your growth journey, you cultivate a spirit of resilience and optimism that paves the way for continued success on the path toward a clutter-free life.

Building Powerful Systems and Routines

In the journey towards maintaining a clutter-free life, building powerful systems and routines is essential for long-term success. These systems and routines act as the backbone of your organized lifestyle, providing structure and stability amidst the hustle and bustle of daily life. They serve as your reliable support system, ensuring that your efforts in decluttering yield lasting results and contribute to an uplifting environment. Creating these systems and routines involves the intentional design of your living spaces, schedules, and habits to facilitate simplicity and order.

One of the key elements in building powerful systems is organization. Establishing designated spaces for items, utilizing storage solutions such as containers and shelves, and implementing a labeling system can streamline your surroundings and make it easier to maintain tidiness. By assigning a specific home for each possession, you cultivate a sense of belonging and purpose for your belongings, reducing the likelihood of clutter accumulation. It also fosters a mindful approach to consumption and acquisition, promoting intentional and meaningful choices when acquiring new items.

Beyond physical organization, the development of daily and weekly routines plays a pivotal role in sustaining a clutter-free lifestyle. Integrating cleaning and decluttering tasks into your regular schedule ensures that maintenance becomes a natural part of your day-to-day activities, rather than an overwhelming chore. Through consistent practices, such as incorporating a 15-minute daily tidying ritual or setting aside a dedicated time each week for decluttering sessions, you proactively prevent clutter from taking root and maintain a harmonious living environment.

Furthermore, integrating technology and digital tools can enhance the efficiency of your organizational systems. Utilizing apps or digital calendars for task management, scheduling reminders for decluttering activities, and digitizing important documents reduce physical clutter while providing convenient access to essential information. Embracing technology empowers you to streamline your administrative tasks and manage your possessions with ease, reinforcing the foundation of a clutter-free lifestyle.

As you construct these robust frameworks within your daily life, remember that flexibility and adaptability are essential components. Life is dynamic, presenting unexpected challenges and changes, and your systems and routines should evolve accordingly. Embrace a growth mindset, viewing adjustments and refinements as opportunities to enhance the effectiveness of your organizational strategies. By remaining open to innovation and improvements, you ensure that your systems and routines continue to meet your evolving needs and aspirations.

Ultimately, the process of building powerful systems and routines reflects your commitment to prioritizing harmony, simplicity, and joy in your everyday life. As you invest in crafting these supportive structures, you empower yourself to navigate through each day with confidence and ease, knowing that your environment is designed to uplift and inspire you.

Nurturing a Clutter-Free Environment

Creating and nurturing a clutter-free environment goes beyond just decluttering physical spaces. It involves curating an atmosphere that promotes peace, clarity, and joy. As you continue on your journey to maintain a clutter-free life, it's important to pay attention to the overall environment in which you live. This encompasses not only your home but also your digital space, your workspace, and even the social circles you engage with. Start by ensuring that every item or aspect in your surroundings adds value to your life in some way. Whether it's a sentimental knickknack, a piece of furniture, or a digital file, each element should contribute positively to your well-being. Consider creating designated zones for different activities within your living space. A tranquil reading nook, an organized work area, or a cozy entertainment zone can enhance the functionality and aesthetic appeal of your environment. Embrace natural light, introduce greenery, and incorporate soothing colors to foster a calming ambiance. Additionally, evaluate your digital environment. Streamline your digital files, unsubscribe from unnecessary newsletters, and declutter your inbox to create a serene virtual space. In your workspace, implement systems that promote efficiency and reduce visual distractions. Cultivate an inspiring and supportive social circle. Surround yourself with individuals who uplift and motivate you, and in turn, offer them the same positive energy. Encourage open communication and meaningful connections that add value to your life while minimizing drama and negativity. Regularly assess and adjust your environment as needed to align with your evolving goals and aspirations. Create a sanctuary where you can thrive and find solace amidst life's challenges. Nurturing a clutter-free environment is a continual process that is integral to sustaining a harmonious and uplifting lifestyle.

Celebrating Your Progress and Success

Congratulations! By coming this far in your decluttering journey, you have taken a significant step toward creating a more fulfilling and organized life. It's essential to pause and celebrate your progress and successes, no matter how small they may seem. Remember, every action and decision you make contributes to the positive transformation happening within your living space and, most importantly, within yourself. Reflect on the changes you've implemented and acknowledge the impact they've had on your daily life. Whether it's as simple as maintaining a clutter-free countertop or organizing a chaotic closet, each accomplishment deserves recognition. Celebrating your progress is a powerful way to reinforce your commitment to this new lifestyle, boosting your confidence and motivation to continue. As part of this celebration, consider expressing gratitude for the improvements you've experienced. Gratitude not only cultivates a positive mindset but also reminds you of the abundance in your life beyond material possessions. Treat yourself to something special—a small reward that symbolizes your dedication and serves as a reminder of how far you've come. Share your achievements with loved ones who support and encourage you. Their acknowledgement will affirm your efforts and contribute to a sense of pride in your accomplishments. Additionally, take the opportunity to appreciate the newfound harmony and peace that your decluttered environment brings. When celebrating your progress, it's also essential to shift your focus from what still needs to be done to what you have already achieved. Embracing a growth-oriented mindset allows you to view your decluttering journey as an ongoing process rather than a destination. Each step forward, no matter how small, is cause for celebration. Finally, remember that your progress and success are not just about the physical changes in your surroundings; they signify a deeper internal transformation. You're creating space for joy, creativity, and serenity in your life. This achievement should be celebrated not just once, but continuously. So, take a moment to revel in your accomplishments, express gratitude, and honor the positive impact you've made on your life and the lives of those around you.

Inspiring Those Around You with Your Journey

One of the most beautiful aspects of embarking on a decluttering journey is the ripple effect it can create. As you gradually transform your surroundings and mindset, those around you can't help but notice the positive changes taking place. Your family, friends, and colleagues become witnesses to your newfound sense of peace and clarity, and this has the potential to inspire them in ways you may not have anticipated.

Your journey serves as a living testament to the transformative power of intentional living. As you share the positive impact of decluttering on your life—both physically and emotionally—you become a beacon of hope for those who may feel overwhelmed by their own cluttered spaces. By openly sharing your challenges, victories, and the joy found in simplicity, you offer a guiding light to others who yearn for similar transformation.

Through your journey, you become an invaluable source of encouragement and motivation for those hesitant to embark on their own path towards a clutter-free life. Your transparency about the obstacles you faced and how you overcame them resonates deeply with others, showing them that change is not only possible but also incredibly rewarding. The anecdotes and insights you offer can help dismantle barriers that have kept others stuck in the cycle of clutter, thereby empowering them to take meaningful steps toward positive change.

Additionally, your willingness to support and uplift those close to you fosters a sense of community and shared purpose. Whether it's offering practical tips on decluttering techniques, recommending life-changing resources, or simply being a compassionate listener, your influence extends far beyond your personal spaces. You showcase the boundless benefits of living with intention and inspire others to reevaluate their own environments and priorities, spurring them to seek out a lighter, more fulfilling way of life.

With every conversation sparked and every insight shared, you plant seeds of possibility in the minds and hearts of those you encounter. Your genuine passion for decluttering and intentional living becomes a catalyst for small shifts in perspective and behavior among your circle of influence. In doing so, you create a network of individuals committed to embracing simplicity and purpose, igniting a collective wave of positive change that extends far beyond what you could achieve alone.

Ultimately, by inspiring those around you with your journey, you contribute to a broader movement of mindful, intentional living. Your influence becomes a legacy of empowerment, guiding numerous individuals toward lives filled with space, tranquility, and the courage to pursue what truly matters.

Visualizing Your Continual Growth and Freedom

As you continue on your journey to a clutter-free life, it's essential to visualize your continual growth and freedom. Imagining the future where your surroundings are uncluttered, and your mind is at peace can be a powerful motivator. Close your eyes and envision a space that is serene, organized, and filled only with items that truly bring you joy. Feel the sense of liberation and harmony that comes with this vision. Allow yourself to bask in the positive emotions that accompany the idea of a perpetually tidy and unburdened existence. This visualization exercise not only serves as inspiration but also reinforces your commitment to maintaining a clutter-free environment. By keeping this image at the forefront of your mind, you will continually reaffirm your dedication to the habits and mindsets that have brought you this far. Visualizing your future state of continual growth and freedom also helps manifest it into reality. The more vividly and frequently you paint this picture in your mind, the more likely you are to attract and create that reality. Stay open to the positive energy and opportunities that will support your journey towards lasting simplicity and order. Embrace the notion that continual growth and freedom are not just aspirational goals—they are tangible, achievable realities within your grasp. Through this visualization, you lay the groundwork for a future that is not only clutter-free but also brimming with innovation, personal development, and limitless possibilities. Every action and decision you make is guided by this clear vision, propelling you forward in your ongoing pursuit of growth and freedom. Remember, the power of visualization lies in its ability to transform aspirations into accomplishments. With each passing day, let your visualized reality of a clutter-free, liberated existence drive you to take deliberate steps in manifesting this ideal future.

As you set your sights on continual growth and freedom, believe wholeheartedly that this vision is not a distant dream but an imminent and sustainable destination that you are actively creating.

Conclusion

As we look back on the 30-day decluttering challenge, it's important to recall the highs and lows of this transformative journey. Reflect on the moments of triumph when you successfully cleared out cluttered spaces, making room for more clarity in your life. Remember the times when motivation waned, and you felt the weight of the challenge. These experiences, both uplifting and difficult, have shaped your growth and resilience. Celebrate your progress with pride, recognizing the determination that led you to this moment. Each day has been an opportunity to uncover new insights about yourself and your relationship with your belongings. Here, you discovered the power of perseverance, realizing that small steps lead to significant change. From navigating sentimental attachments to managing practical items, each decision echoes a commitment to embracing a clutter-free life. In this recap, honor the effort you put into making lasting improvements. When challenges arose, you found strength within yourself to push forward, further solidifying your ability to overcome obstacles. Embrace the lessons learned throughout the 30 days, gaining a deeper understanding of what truly holds value in your life. By acknowledging the hurdles you faced, you reinforce the resilience that propels you towards continued success. Take pride in the transformation you've achieved and how it has positively impacted your surroundings and mindset. The 30-day challenge has served as a catalyst for personal growth, empowering you to confront clutter head-on and emerge victorious. As you embrace your achievements, bask in the realization that these pivotal moments have laid a foundation for a brighter, more organized future.

Living a clutter-free life goes beyond simply having an organized physical space; it brings forth a multitude of rewards that positively impact every aspect of your being. As you embark on this journey, it's essential to recognize the incredible benefits that await you. Firstly, imagine waking up in a serene and tidy environment every morning. A clutter-free home promotes a sense of calm and tranquility, setting the tone for a peaceful and focused day ahead.

Furthermore, decluttering allows you to reclaim precious time that was once lost searching through chaos. With everything in its place, you'll find yourself more efficient and productive, leading to a greater sense of accomplishment. The positive energy that flows from a clutter-free space enables you to tackle challenges with clarity and determination.

Beyond the physical realm, the emotional and mental benefits of decluttering are profound. Letting go of unnecessary possessions and mental burdens creates space for joy, contentment, and creativity to flourish. You'll find yourself experiencing deeper connections with loved ones and fostering a stronger sense of gratitude for the beauty in everyday life.

In addition to personal well-being, a clutter-free life can also positively impact your financial health. By streamlining your possessions and making conscious decisions about what truly matters, you'll find yourself spending less on unnecessary purchases and investing in experiences or items of genuine value.

Moreover, the ripple effect of decluttering extends to your professional life. A clutter-free mind and environment pave the way for enhanced focus, innovation, and strategic thinking, thus leading to increased opportunities and success in your career.

Finally, living clutter-free empowers you to lead by example and inspire others to embark on their own transformative journeys. Your newfound lightness and vitality become a beacon of hope, encouraging those around you to embrace positive changes and pursue their aspirations with renewed vigor.

In embracing and celebrating the benefits of a clutter-free life, you open the door to a world of endless possibilities, inner peace, and boundless enthusiasm. Your decision to declutter is not just a physical act but a powerful affirmation of self-love, intentionality, and the limitless potential within you.

Keeping the Flame Alive - Maintaining Momentum Beyond the Challenge

As you reach the conclusion of the 30-day decluttering challenge, it's important to focus on sustaining the positive changes you've made in your life. Keeping the flame alive means nurturing the newfound sense of clarity and joy that comes with a clutter-free environment. It's about creating a lasting impact that goes beyond the initial excitement of transformation. How can you ensure that the momentum gained during the challenge continues to propel you forward? Firstly, it's vital to acknowledge the value of what you've accomplished. Recognize the effort you've invested and the progress you've made. Celebrate each small victory, as they collectively contribute to a significant change in your lifestyle. Reflect on the positive effects of decluttering - the enhanced productivity, increased serenity, and improved overall well-being. Embrace this as motivation to keep moving forward. Continuing this journey involves integrating the habits and mindsets you've cultivated into your daily life. As you transition from the challenge phase to the long-term maintenance phase, establish a sustainable routine that incorporates the principles of decluttering. This may involve setting aside dedicated time for organizing, reinforcing positive behaviors, and being mindful of what items enter your space. Engage in activities that align with your clutter-free values, such as mindfulness practices, regular purging sessions, and conscious consumer habits. Stay connected with the supportive community you've built during the challenge. Surround yourself with individuals who share your commitment to a clutter-free life and draw strength from their encouragement. Share your experiences, challenges, and successes, and uplift others in their journey. By contributing to a collective spirit of positivity and growth, you reinforce your own dedication and resilience. Look ahead with a mindset of continuous improvement. Set new goals and aspirations that expand upon the foundation you've established. Whether it's further simplifying your living space, exploring minimalist philosophies, or extending the benefits of decluttering to other areas of your life, envision a future filled with possibilities. Embrace the freedom and empowerment that come from maintaining a clutter-free existence. Remember, this is not just a one-time accomplishment, but an ongoing commitment to personal fulfillment. In fostering a clutter-free lifestyle, you're nurturing a profound sense of contentment and harmony. Your journey doesn't end with the 30-day challenge – it's a lifelong adventure of intentional living and untold possibilities. By embracing the principles of decluttering, you're igniting a flame of positivity and transformation that will continue to illuminate your path, guiding you toward a brighter, more uplifting future.

As you stand amidst the serenity of your newly decluttered environment, take a moment to bask in the profound transformation you've undergone. This isn't just about tidying up physical spaces; it's about nurturing your mind and spirit. Reflect on the person you were when you started this journey—the doubt, hesitation, and perhaps even skepticism that once clouded your thoughts. Now, envision the empowered and invigorated individual before you today. Take pride in the courage it took to embark on this path towards rejuvenation. By choosing to confront and conquer clutter, you've unlocked an unparalleled potential for growth and self-discovery. Every item discarded represents a triumph over attachment and fear; every space cleared signifies a leap towards unyielding clarity and purpose. Embrace the awe-inspiring metamorphosis that has taken place within you. You are not just decluttered—you are transformed. Your newfound lightness extends beyond the material realm, permeating through every facet of your existence. Your relationships flourish with renewed vigor, unencumbered by the weight of unnecessary possessions. Your mind, once crowded with distractions, now revels in the spaciousness and tranquility of a clutter-free sanctuary. Celebrate the resilience and dedication that have brought you to this point. Recognize the depth of strength and determination that course through your being. Today, you stand as a testament to the extraordinary power of intentional living. Cherish this moment of reflection, for it is a testament to your unwavering commitment to personal growth and an affirmation of the boundless potential that resides within you.

Amidst the joy of celebrating your transformation and the excitement of setting new goals for continuous improvement, it's important to emphasize the significance of commitment to clarity. This represents the anchor that holds your newfound clutter-free lifestyle in place, ensuring that you stay focused on the path you've embarked upon. Commitment to clarity is about being resolute in your decision to lead a clutter-free life, understanding the deep-seated reasons behind this choice, and aligning your daily actions with this vision.

Staying true to your new lifestyle involves embracing the essence of simplicity and mindfulness. It requires a conscious effort to resist the temptation of reverting to old habits and patterns that once led to clutter. Consider this as an opportunity to redefine your relationship with material possessions, mental clutter, and even toxic relationships. By nurturing a commitment to clarity, you are not just tidying up your physical space; you are fostering a mindset of empowerment and intentional living.

As you navigate this journey, remember that commitment to clarity extends beyond the realm of decluttering. It permeates every aspect of your life, shaping your decisions, interactions, and aspirations. Choose to surround yourself with individuals who uplift and inspire you on this path, and reciprocate their positivity. Release any lingering doubts or fears and welcome the abundance of opportunities that await you. Stay open to growth and adaptability while maintaining the steadfast commitment to clarity that you've embraced.

It's natural to encounter challenges along the way, questioning the choices you've made and the commitments you've pledged. During these moments, reflect on the profound impact that decluttering has had on your life. Recall the mental and emotional liberation you've experienced, the sense of renewed purpose, and the freedom to design the life you desire. Let these reflections fortify your commitment to clarity and serve as beacons of inspiration in the face of uncertainty.

Finally, staying true to your new lifestyle necessitates an unwavering belief in the transformative power of clarity. Embrace each day as an opportunity to reinforce your commitment, to illuminate the intrinsic beauty of simplicity, and to radiate positivity to those around you. Through this devotion, you create a ripple effect far beyond your personal sphere, influencing others to embark on their own path towards clarity. So, reaffirm your determination, bask in the serenity of your clutter-free sanctuary, and celebrate the lifelong commitment to clarity that has ignited profound change within you.

Visioning Forward - Setting New Goals for Continuous Improvement

As you embrace the transformative power of decluttering and commit to maintaining a clutter-free lifestyle, it's essential to continue setting new goals for continuous improvement. Visioning forward allows you to harness the momentum gained from your decluttering journey and channel it into an even brighter, more fulfilling future.

Setting new goals is an invigorating process that keeps you motivated and focused. Start by reflecting on how far you've come since embarking on the decluttering challenge. Take pride in the positive changes you've experienced and let them inspire your vision for the future. Visualize the life you aspire to lead – one that is unencumbered by clutter, both physical and mental, and filled with purpose, joy, and abundance.

Next, consider the areas in which you'd like to see further improvement. Perhaps you want to cultivate a deeper sense of mindfulness, build stronger connections in your relationships, or pursue new passions and hobbies. Whatever your aspirations may be, set specific, attainable goals that align with your newfound clarity and freedom. Remember, these goals are not just about removing physical clutter; they're about enhancing every aspect of your life.

Alongside setting new goals, it's crucial to establish an action plan to bring them to fruition. Break down your broader objectives into manageable steps and create a timeline for achieving them. Whether it's dedicating time each day to introspection and gratitude, scheduling regular outings with loved ones, or investing in activities that bring you fulfillment, every action propels you toward a brighter and more vibrant future.

As you embark on this journey of continuous improvement, remain open to adaptation and growth. Life is dynamic, and your goals can evolve alongside you. Embrace the agility to adjust your plans as needed and maintain an optimistic outlook. Encountering setbacks or challenges along the way is natural, but your resilient spirit has already proven itself through the decluttering process. With newfound determination, face each obstacle with creativity, positivity, and an unwavering belief in your ability to overcome.

In crafting your vision for the future, strive for balance and harmony in all aspects of your life. Your goals should encompass not only your immediate surroundings but also your emotional well-being, personal growth, and contribution to the world around you. By setting holistic, transformative goals, you continue to manifest the life you desire and deserve.

Remember, with each step you take towards your new goals, cherish the progress you've made and celebrate the person you are becoming. The journey of continuous improvement is a testament to your resilience, strength, and unwavering commitment to living a clutter-free, purposeful life.

Creating a clutter-free life is not just about decluttering physical spaces; it's also about cultivating daily habits that support your journey towards simplicity and serenity. These simple practices form the foundation for maintaining a clutter-free lifestyle, ensuring that the progress you've made stays with you for the long term. One of the most effective daily habits for success in staying clutter-free is practicing mindfulness. By being present in the moment, you can make conscious decisions about what you allow into your life, whether physical belongings, digital clutter, or even negative thoughts. Embracing mindfulness empowers you to appreciate the joy of living with less and the freedom it brings. Another crucial habit involves setting aside dedicated time each day for tidying up and organizing. Whether it's a quick 10-minute tidy session in the morning or an evening routine to ensure everything is in its place before bed, this consistent practice prevents clutter from building up again. Moreover, incorporating gratitude into your daily routine fosters a positive mindset and reinforces the value of what you already have, reducing the impulse to accumulate unnecessary possessions. Expressing gratitude for the simplicity and order in your life amplifies the satisfaction of maintaining a clutter-free space. Additionally, creating a system for handling incoming items is vital. Whether it's sorting mail as soon as it arrives, clearing out your email inbox regularly, or evaluating potential purchases against your true needs, having a strategy in place stops clutter at its source. Lastly, connecting with a community that shares your values and goals can provide invaluable support on your clutter-free journey. Engaging with like-minded individuals through social media groups, local meetups, or online forums offers encouragement, inspiration, and practical tips for staying organized. Surrounding yourself with a support system that understands and champions your commitment to simplicity reinforces your dedication to a clutter-free life. By embracing these daily habits, you'll build resilience against the reemergence of clutter and nurture a sustainable mindset focused on the peace and purpose of a clutter-free existence.

Picture this: You've spent the last 30 days decluttering your life, and now, as you bask in the glowing aura of accomplishment, you realize the power of surrounding yourself with encouraging individuals. A support system can be a driving force in helping you maintain the positive changes you've made. It's about establishing a network of like-minded friends, family members, or even online communities that lift you up and keep you motivated on your clutter-free journey. Your support system should be filled with people who understand and appreciate your achievement and are there to cheer you on without judgment. Whether it's a friend who celebrates your decision to let go of material possessions or a family member who acknowledges your commitment to a simpler lifestyle, these individuals play a crucial role in reinforcing your efforts. Surrounding yourself with encouragement is not just about receiving praise; it's also about having access to guidance and inspiration whenever you need it. Seek out mentors or role models who have successfully embraced a clutter-free life. Their experiences and advice can provide invaluable insights and help you navigate any challenges that may come your way. Additionally, consider joining support groups or online forums dedicated to decluttering and minimalist living. Engaging with individuals who share similar goals can create a sense of community and mutual support, offering you a platform to exchange ideas, seek advice, and celebrate milestones together. Remember, building a support system isn't just about receiving encouragement; it's also about spreading positivity and inspiration to others. Your journey towards a clutter-free life can serve as motivation for those around you, inspiring them to embark on their own transformative paths.

Take pride in being a source of encouragement and empowerment for others, and in turn, watch as your support system grows stronger and more dynamic. By nurturing positive connections and surrounding yourself with individuals who champion your aspirations, you're fortifying your resolve and creating an environment conducive to sustained success. Through these genuine relationships, you'll discover the unmatched power of encouragement in navigating your clutter-free life with unwavering determination and joyous enthusiasm.

As you approach the final stages of your decluttering journey, it's vital to take a moment to reflect on how far you've come. The process may have been challenging at times, but the rewards are evident, and each step taken has led to this pivotal point. Reflect on the significant changes you've witnessed in your surroundings, your mindset, and even your relationships. Take time to rejoice in the newfound sense of freedom and lightness that comes with a clutter-free life. Celebrate the small wins and the big victories because each one has contributed to this transformative experience.

Appreciating your journey involves acknowledging the courage it took to confront your clutter head-on and the determination it required to persevere through the more difficult moments. It's about recognizing the growth you've undergone, the lessons you've learned, and the positive impact your dedication has had on yourself and those around you. Embrace gratitude for the support system that stood by you and provided encouragement during the tough times. Remember the inspiring messages and stories that motivated you to keep going and never lose sight of your goal.

Rejoicing in your journey doesn't mean the end of progress; it signifies a significant milestone in your ongoing pursuit of a clutter-free, harmonious life. Look back on the memories created throughout this process and the experiences that have shaped your personal development. Acknowledge the way your perspective has evolved and the clarity that now permeates every aspect of your life. Use these reflections to propel yourself forward as you carry the spirit of perseverance and gratitude into the next phase of your journey.

Taking time to appreciate your journey allows you to bask in the positivity and fulfillment that accompany every triumph along the way. It sets the stage for new beginnings and inspires confidence as you continue to navigate the path of self-improvement and happiness. So, take a deep breath, reflect on how incredibly far you've come, and rejoice in the transformation that has unfolded. Your journey towards a clutter-free life has not only reshaped your external environment but has also kindled a vibrant, exuberant spirit within you. Be proud of your resilience and zest for embracing change. You are now ready to step into the beautiful possibilities that await you.

Inspiring Words - Embrace the Freedom of a Clutter-Free Life

Embracing the freedom of a clutter-free life is a truly transformative experience that opens doors to new opportunities and a sense of liberation that words can hardly capture. As you have journeyed through the decluttering process and embraced the essence of simplicity, you have embarked on a path towards a brighter, more joyful existence. It's essential to recognize that the liberation from physical, mental, and emotional clutter is not merely about tidying up your surroundings; it is about liberating your spirit.

As you stand in your decluttered space, take a moment to inhale the newfound freedom. The absence of chaos allows you to breathe a little easier, think a little clearer, and live a little fuller. Look around and soak in the tranquility that now emanates from your home. This serenity echoes within you, becoming a source of inspiration for the journey ahead. Your decluttered environment serves as a canvas where you can paint the picture of the life you've always dreamed of living.

Each item you choose to retain holds purpose and beauty, contributing positively to your life. Every open space represents the limitless potential that awaits you. It's a sanctuary that nurtures your creativity, your passions, and your genuine self. From this point on, your world is defined not by excess but by intentionality, not by stress but by ease, and not by clutter but by clarity.

All the energy once spent on managing possessions and distractions can now be redirected towards pursuits that light your soul on fire. With each step forward, savor the empowered feeling of shedding layers of unnecessary weight, making way for boundless opportunities. In embracing the freedom of a clutter-free life, you step into a realm where simplicity is the keynote, gratitude is the anthem, and love for oneself and others envelops every corner.

The joy of living with less is not in deprivation but in abundance—a surplus of peace, purpose, and presence. As you continue on this fulfilling path, remember that it's not about achieving perfection; it's about relishing the journey and constantly aligning your life with what truly matters. Let your heart dance with the rhythm of simplicity, and let your spirit revel in the euphoria of being unburdened and unshackled from the weight of excess.

Today, tomorrow, and for all the days to come, may you hold steadfast to the promise of a clutter-free life—a life where the beauty of simplicity continually unfolds, and every moment is an opportunity to thrive, inspire, and radiate the purest version of yourself.

Thank You

Just wanted to let you know how much you mean to me.

Without your help and attention, I couldn't keep making helpful publications like this one.

Once again, I appreciate you reading this book. I absolutely enjoyed writing it, and I hope you did too.

Before you leave, I need you to do me a favor.

Please consider posting a book review for this one on the platform.

Reviews will be used to help my writing.

Your feedback is extremely helpful to me and will help me to generate more. upcoming books in the information genre.

I would love to hear from you.

Seraphine Silverwood.